Bursting at the Seams

Bursting at the Seams

A **wealth** of **wit** and **wisdom**
by, for and
about **women**

Killy John & Alie Stibbe

MONARCH
BOOKS
Oxford, UK & Grand Rapids, Michigan, USA

First published in the UK in 2004 by Monarch Books
(a publishing imprint of Lion Hudson plc),
Mayfield House, 256 Banbury Road, Oxford OX2 7DH
Tel: +44 (0) 1865 302750 Fax: +44 (0) 1865 302757
Email: monarch@lionhudson.com
www.lionhudson.com

Illustrations by Doreen Lang

UK ISBN 1 85424 653 4
US ISBN 0 8254 6065 4

Distributed by:
UK: Marston Book Services Ltd, PO Box 269,
Abingdon, Oxon OX14 4YN;
USA: Kregel Publications, PO Box 2607,
Grand Rapids, Michigan 49501.

British Library Cataloguing Data
A catalogue record for this book is available
from the British Library.

Book design and production for the publishers by
Gazelle Creative Productions Ltd,
Concorde House, Grenville Place, Mill Hill, London NW7 3SA.
Printed in Malta.

Acknowledgements

Thanks to all those who have given us permission to use material reproduced in this collection. Every effort has been made to trace original copyright holders where required; though in some cases this has proved impossible. We shall be happy to correct any such omissions in future editions.

Thanks to Karen Oberst, who gave us unprecedented access to quotes by women published on her website.

And thanks especially to our husbands, John and Mark, for their support, patience, and proofreading!

Note to church magazine editors

Introduction

When we first had the idea of compiling a book of women's humour, we had no idea what we were letting ourselves in for; we thought it would be a simple, quick, cut-and-paste operation. That was our first tactic, but our best critics (our husbands!) put a red pen through the whole lot – it was unprintable – and we burnt it! Only then did we realise what an awful lot of incredibly bad women's humour there is; most of it not only goes out of the way to put men down, but puts women down in the process. So it was back to the drawing board. This time we realised that, as Christians, we needed to produce a book that celebrated the differences between the sexes without being afraid to laugh at those differences, and yet provoked constructive thought.

We ended up with what we would like to think of as a compilation of wit and wisdom that might appeal to women from different backgrounds, at different stages of life, and in a multitude of different circumstances. We have deliberately tried to keep any quotes we have used to those made by women about issues relating to women. However, we have included some quotes by men about women's issues, because we felt these were particularly informative or insightful – and it's always good to see things from another perspective.

In the film *Forrest Gump*, Tom Hanks said, "Life is like a box of chocolates and you never know quite what you're gonna get." It's probably the same with *Bursting at the Seams*. We're presenting you with a gift-wrapped selection: dark and light, soft-centred and hard-centred, some of which you will like, and some of which you might want to spit right out! But, just like the gift-wrapped box of chocolates, the thought is there – and in the same way, this book is our gift to you. Enjoy!

Killy and Alie, April 2004

A

ABILITY

I've got a woman's ability to stick to a job and get on with it when everyone else walks off and leaves it.

Margaret Thatcher

Everyone has inside them a piece of good news.
The good news is you don't know how great you can be!
How much you can love!
What you can accomplish!
And what your potential is!

Anne Frank

There are only three colours, ten digits and seven notes; it is what we do with them that is important.

Ruth Ross

It is the ability to choose which makes us human.

Madeleine l'Engle

Everyone has talent. What is rare is the courage to follow that talent to the... place where it leads.

Erica Jong

ACCEPTANCE

Acceptance is what we wish for ourselves and often deny others.

Susan L. Taylor

ACCEPT: the secret of a good marriage

Attraction
Communication
Commitment
Enjoyment
Purpose
Trust

Source unknown

ACHIEVEMENT

If you think you're too small to have an impact, try going to bed with a mosquito.

Anita Roddick

There are three ways you can get to the top of a tree:

1) sit on an acorn
2) make friends with a bird
3) climb it.

Anon.

I can do no great things, only small things with great love.

Mother Teresa

I am only one; but still I am one.
I cannot do everything, but still I can do something.
I will not refuse to do the something I can do.

Helen Keller

All great achievements require time.

Anne Frank

Remember, Ginger Rogers did everything that Fred Astaire did, but she did it backwards and in high heels.

Faith Whittlesey

You must do the thing you think you cannot do.

Eleanor Roosevelt

If I could give you information of my life it would be to show how a woman of very ordinary ability has been led by God in strange and unaccustomed paths to do in his service what he has done in her. And if I could tell you all, you would see how God has done all, and I nothing. I have worked hard, very hard, that is all; and I have never refused God anything.

Florence Nightingale

For what is done or learned by one class of women becomes, by virtue of their common womanhood, the property of all women.

Elizabeth Blackwell
(The first woman in the US to become a doctor.)

Achievements bring their own anticlimax.

Agatha Christie,
They came to Baghdad

How do you benefit if you gain the whole world but lose your own soul in the process?

Jesus Christ, *The Bible*,
Matthew 16:26

So celebrate what you've accomplished, but raise the bar a little higher each time you succeed.

Mia Hamm

ACTION

We won't always know whose lives we touched and made better for our having cared, because actions can sometimes have unforeseen ramifications. What's important is that you do care and you act.

Charlotte Lunsford

I never see what has been done;
I only see what remains to be done.

Marie Curie

If you want anything said, ask a man.
If you want anything done, ask a woman.

Margaret Thatcher

Men have the grand vision, and they pass it on to somebody else to put into practice. Women follow the details more; they want to know that it is being put into practice.

Mary Eugenia Charles,
Prime Minister, Commonwealth of Dominica

Let us stop just saying we love each other;
let us really show it by our actions.

***The Bible*, 1 John 3:18**

Because you are able to do it and because you have a right to do it, doesn't mean you have to do it.

Dr Laura Schlesinger

ADVICE

The best way to give advice is to set a good example.

Anon.

Advice is what we ask for when we already know the answer but wish we didn't.

Erica Jong

Advice for life

The best thing to give
– to your enemy is forgiveness;
– to an opponent, tolerance;
– to a friend, your ear;
– to your child, good example;
– to your father, reverence;
– to your mother, conduct that will make her proud of you;
– to yourself, respect;
– to all people, charity.

Benjamin Franklin

Timely advice is as lovely as golden apples in a silver basket. Valid criticism is as treasured by the one who heeds it as jewellery made from finest gold.

***The Bible*, Proverbs 25:11–12**

Everyone likes to give advice, but no one likes to take it.

Anon.

I give myself, sometimes, admirable advice, but I am incapable of taking it.

Lady Mary Wortley Montagu

Advice from children

Proverbs are always a useful source of advice and wisdom. A teacher gave the children in her class the first half of some proverbs, and asked them to come up with the remainder... their insight was illuminating!

Strike while the... bug is close.
It's always darkest before... they put the clocks forward.
Never underestimate the power of... termites.
You can lead a horse to water... but how?
Don't bite the hand... that looks dirty.
No news is... impossible.
A miss is as good as a... Mr.
You can't teach an old dog new... maths problems.
If you lie down with dogs, you... stink in the morning.
Love all, trust... me.
The pen is mightier than the... pigs.
An idle mind is... the best way to relax.
Where there's smoke there's... pollution.
Happy is the bride who... gets all the presents.
A penny saved is... not much.
Two's company, three's... the Musketeers.
Don't put off till tomorrow what... you put on to go to bed.
Laugh and the whole world laughs with you, cry and... you have to blow your nose.
If at first you don't succeed... get new batteries.
You get out of something... what you see on the box.

The true secret of giving advice is, after you have honestly given it, to be perfectly indifferent whether it is taken or not, and never persist in trying to set people right.
Hannah Whitall Smith

AGE

From birth to age 18 a girl needs good parents. From 18 to 35 she needs good looks. From 35 to 55 she needs a good personality. From 55 on, she needs good cash.

Sophie Tucker (1884–1966), American singer

Old age is the verdict of life.

Amelia Barr

I dread no more the first white in my hair,
Or even age itself, the easy shoe,
The cane, the wrinkled hands, the special chair
Time, doing this to me, may alter too
My sorrow, into something I can bear.

Edna St Vincent Millay

Three old women were sitting around a table talking. The first said, "I'm getting so forgetful; I was standing at the top of the stairs and I couldn't remember whether I was going down or had just come up."

The second woman said, "You think that's bad? The other day I was sitting on my bed and I couldn't remember whether I was going to sleep or getting up."

The third woman smiled smugly, and rapped the table, saying, "Well, I have no memory problems at all!" After a moment of silence she looked round and asked, "Who's there?"

A woman never forgets her age – once she decides what it is.

Source unknown

A capable wife... is clothed with strength and dignity, and she laughs with no fear of the future.

***The Bible*, Proverbs 31:10, 25**

Years wrinkle the skin, but to give up enthusiasm wrinkles the soul.

Source unknown

The great thing about getting older is that you don't lose all the other ages you've been.

Madeleine l'Engle

It is so comic to hear oneself called old, even at 90, I suppose!

Alice James

Women may be the one group that grows more radical with age.

Gloria Steinem

You can judge your age by the amount of pain you feel when you come in contact with a new idea... Perhaps one has to be very old before one learns to be amused rather than shocked.

Pearl S. Buck

The hardest years in life are those between ten and seventy.

Helen Hayes

A woman has the age she deserves.

Coco Chanel

Being an old maid is like death by drowning – a really delightful sensation after you have ceased struggling.

Edna Ferber

Age does not protect you from love, but love to some extent protects you from age.

Jeanne Moreau

One of the signs of passing youth is the birth of a sense of fellowship with other human beings as we take our place among them.

Virginia Woolf

I'm not interested in age. People who tell me their age are silly. You're as old as you feel.

Elizabeth Arden

Age is no barrier. It's a limitation you put on your mind.

Jackie Joyner-Kersee

AIMS and AMBITION

A strange ambition for a girl...

On returning from a meeting of the American National Organisation for Women, Meg Quijano was met by her five-year-old daughter. The little girl told her that when she grew up she wanted to be a nurse. Not wanting her daughter to limit herself to a job that was perceived as "female", Meg told her daughter she could be anything she wanted to – a lawyer, a surgeon, a banker, even President. The girl looked doubtful. "Anything?" she said. "Yes," said her mother. "Then I want to be a HORSE!"

Don't be selfish; don't live to make a good impression on others. Be humble, thinking of others as better than yourself. Don't think only about your own affairs, but be interested in others, too, and what they are doing.

***The Bible*, Philippians 2:3–4**

Most people want to improve themselves, but not many want to work at it.

Anon.

Very few people are ambitious in the sense of having a specific image of what they want to achieve. Most people's sights are only toward the next rung, the next increment of money.

Judith M. Bardwick

A person who gets ahead by oppressing the poor or by showering gifts on the rich will end in poverty.

***The Bible*, Proverbs 22:16**

A soul without a high aim is like a ship without a rudder.

Eileen Caddy

ANGER

Anger is one letter short of danger.

Source unknown

Anger can be a very positive thing, the thing that moves us beyond the acceptance of evil.

Joan Chittister

Don't sin by letting anger gain control over you. Do not let the sun go down while you are still angry.

***The Bible*, Ephesians 4:26–27**

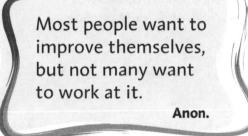

And my granny told me: "When you grow up and get married, darling, always have a double bed. You can never keep on quarrelling if you can reach out and touch each other."

Jilly Cooper, *Daily Mail*, 31 May 2003

Ask yourself, "What difference will this thing we're fighting about make in ten years? In one year? In a month?"

Source unknown

ANNIVERSARIES

On Valentine's Day

An old man got on a bus one 14th February, carrying a dozen roses. He sat beside a young man. The young man looked at the roses and said, "Somebody's going to get a beautiful Valentine's Day gift."

"Yes," said the old man.

A few minutes went by and the old man noticed that his young companion was staring at the roses. "Do you have a girlfriend?" the old man asked.

"I do," said the young man. "I'm going to see her right now, and I'm going to give her this Valentine's Day card."

They rode in silence for another ten minutes, and then the old man got up to get off the bus. As he stepped out into the aisle, he suddenly placed the roses on the young man's lap and said, "I think my wife would want you to have these. I'll tell her that I gave them to you."

He left the bus quickly. As the bus pulled away, the young man turned to see the old man enter the gates of a cemetery.

Source unknown

A man and his wife in their 60s were celebrating their 40th wedding anniversary. Their guardian angels appeared to them and said that because they had been such a devoted couple they could each be granted a special request.

The wife wished for a trip around the world with her husband, and lo and behold, she immediately had the cruise tickets and documentation in her hands.

The husband saw what she had got and wished for a female companion 30 years younger.

Immediately he turned 90!

Appearances can be deceiving…

A woman in a faded dress and her husband, dressed in a threadbare suit, stepped off the train in Boston, and walked timidly without an appointment into the Harvard University President's outer office.

The secretary could tell in a moment that this couple had no business at Harvard.

"We would like to see the President of Harvard," the man said softly.

"He'll be busy all day," the secretary snapped. "We'll wait," the woman replied. For hours the secretary ignored them, hoping that the couple would finally become discouraged and go away. They didn't and the secretary grew frustrated and finally decided to disturb the President, even though it was something she always regretted.

"Maybe if you see them for a few minutes, they'll leave," she said to him.

He sighed in exasperation and nodded. Someone of his importance obviously didn't have the time to spend with this odd couple. The President, stern faced, strutted toward the couple.

The woman told him, "We had a son who attended Harvard for one year. He loved Harvard. He was happy here. But about a year ago, he died in an accident. My husband and I would like to erect a memorial to him, somewhere on the campus."

The President wasn't touched… he was shocked.

"Madam," he said, gruffly, "we can't put up a statue for every person who attended Harvard and died. If we did, this place would look like a cemetery." "Oh, no," the woman explained quickly. "We don't want to erect a statue. We thought we would like to give a building to Harvard." The President rolled his eyes. He glanced at the woman's faded dress and the man's threadbare suit, and then exclaimed, "A building! Do you have any earthly idea how much a building costs? We have over seven and a half million dollars in the physical buildings here at Harvard." For a moment the woman was silent.

The President was pleased. Maybe he could get rid of them now. The woman turned to her husband and said quietly, "Is that all it costs to start a university? Why don't we just start our own?" Her husband nodded.

The President's face wilted in confusion and bewilderment. Mr and Mrs Leland Stanford got up and walked away. They moved to Palo Alto in California where they established the university that bears their and their son's name, Stanford University.

APPRECIATION

Appreciation can make a day –
even change a life.
Your willingness to put it into
words is all that is necessary.
Margaret Cousins

ASPIRATIONS

Far away there in the sunshine are my highest aspirations. I may not reach them, but I can look up and see their beauty, believe in them, and try to follow where they lead.
Louisa May Alcott

I want to be all that I am capable of becoming.
Katherine Mansfield

It would be as wise to set up an accomplished lawyer to saw wood as a business as to condemn an educated and sensible woman to spend all her time boiling potatoes and patching old garments. Yet this is the lot of many a one who incessantly stitches and boils and bakes, compelled to thrust back out of sight the aspirations which fill her soul.
Sarah Grimke

ATTITUDE

Work is either fun or drudgery – it depends on your attitude.

Colleen C. Barrett

The greatest part of our happiness depends on our dispositions, not our circumstances.

Martha Washington

The remarkable thing we have, is a choice every day regarding the attitude we will embrace for that day. We cannot change our past.... We cannot change the fact that people will act in a certain way. We cannot change the inevitable. The only thing we can do is play on the one string we have, and that is our attitude.

Charles Swindoll

Instead of looking at life as a narrowing funnel, we can see it ever widening to choose the things we want to do, to take the wisdom we've learned and create something.

Liz Carpenter

Nothing in life is so hard that you can't make it easier by the way you take it.

Ellen Glasgow

I am convinced that attitude is the key to success or failure in almost any of life's endeavours. Your attitude – your perspective, your outlook, how you feel about yourself, how you feel about other people – determines your priorities, your actions, your values. Your attitude determines how you interact with other people and how you interact with yourself.

Carolyn Warner

BABIES

Being a mother changes with each baby…

Here are some of the ways having a second, third and fourth child is different from having the first.

Your clothes
1st baby: You begin wearing maternity clothes as soon as your doctor confirms your pregnancy.
2nd baby: You wear your regular clothes for as long as possible.
3rd baby: Your maternity clothes *are* your regular clothes.
4th baby: Borrow your friend's maternity clothes – yours have worn out.

Preparing for the birth
1st baby: You practise your breathing daily.
2nd baby: You don't bother practising because you remember that last time, breathing didn't do a thing to ease the pain.
3rd baby: You ask for an epidural as soon as you arrive in hospital.
4th baby: You're lucky if you make it to the hospital – as you're too busy making tea for three other children.

The baby's clothes
1st baby: You pre-wash your newborn's clothes, colour-co-ordinate them, and fold them neatly away.
2nd baby: You check to make sure that the clothes are clean and discard only the ones with serious stains.
3rd baby: Boys can wear pink, can't they?
4th baby: All the baby clothes are worn out, so you borrow your friend's old baby clothes.

Worries
1st baby: At the first sign of distress – a whimper, a frown – you pick up the baby.
2nd baby: You pick the baby up when he/she wails so loudly that he/she might wake up the firstborn.
3rd baby: You teach your three-year-old how to rewind the mechanical swing while you jiggle no. 2.
4th baby: You don't notice the attachment to your hip that makes you stand so awkwardly

the whole time and restricts tasks to the use of one hand.

Dummy

1st baby: If the dummy falls on the floor, you put it away until you can go home to wash and boil it.
2nd baby: When the dummy falls on the floor, you squirt it off with some milk from the baby's bottle.
3rd baby: You wipe it off on your jeans and pop it back in.
4th baby: Sucks on the sink plunger.

Nappies

1st baby: You change your baby's nappy every hour, whether they need it or not.
2nd baby: You change their nappy every four hours, if needed.
3rd baby: You try to change their nappy before others start to complain about the smell or you see it sagging to their knees.
4th baby: Nappies? What are they?

Activities

1st baby: You take your child to Tumble Tots and Baby Story Hour.
2nd baby: You take your children to Tumble Tots and Toddler Group.
3rd baby: You take your children to the supermarket.
4th baby: You drop your three children at nursery, take your baby to college and register yourself for a course, any course...

Going out

1st baby: The first time you leave your baby with a baby-sitter, you phone home ten times.
2nd baby: Just before you walk out the door, you remember to leave a number where you can be reached.
3rd baby: You leave instructions for the sitter to call only if the house is on fire.
4th baby: Can you find someone who will sit for four under-fives?

At home

1st baby: You spend much of each day just gazing at the baby.
2nd baby: You spend a bit of every day watching to be sure your older child isn't squeezing, poking or hitting the baby.
3rd baby: You spend a little bit of every day hiding from the children.
4th baby: You realise this is it – childhood rushes by so fast that you're going to find the balance and enjoy *all* your children while they still want to know you.

Never quarrel about a baby's name before it is born.

Norwegian proverb

Can a mother forget her nursing child? Can she feel no love for a child she has borne?

***The Bible*, Isaiah 49:15**

When you have a baby, you set off an explosion in your marriage, and when the dust settles, your marriage is different from what it was. Not better, necessarily: not worse, necessarily; but different.

Nora Ephron

BEAUTY

You can take no credit for beauty at sixteen. But if you are beautiful at sixty, it will be your own soul's doing.

Marie Stopes

People are like stained-glass windows. They sparkle and shine when the sun is out, but when the darkness sets in their true beauty is revealed only if there is a light from within.

Elisabeth Kübler-Ross

The best and most beautiful things in the world cannot be seen or even touched – they must be felt with the heart.

Helen Keller

It's beauty that captures your attention; but personality that captures your heart.

Anon.

BEAUTY IS IN THE EYE OF THE BEHOLDER

So much has been said and sung of beautiful young girls, why doesn't somebody wake up to the beauty of older women?

Harriet Beecher Stowe

Don't be concerned about the outward beauty that depends on fancy hairstyles, expensive jewellery or beautiful clothes. You should be known for the beauty that comes from within; the unfading beauty of a gentle and quiet spirit, which is so precious to God.

***The Bible*, 1 Peter 3:3–4**

Why should not a woman be like nature, sometimes spring, sometimes autumn, now summer, now winter?

Elizabeth Prentiss

People see you as an object, not as a person, and they project a set of expectations onto you. People who don't have it think beauty is a blessing, but actually it sets you apart.

Candice Bergen

BEGINNINGS

Don't wait for something big to occur. Start where you are, with what you have, and that will always lead you into something greater.

Mary Manin Morrissey

Begin somewhere; you cannot build a reputation on what you intend to do.

Liz Smith

The world is round and the place which may seem like the end may also be the beginning.

Ivy Baker Priest

BEREAVEMENT

The Lord is close to the broken-hearted;
he rescues those who are crushed in spirit.

The Bible, Psalm 34:18

The bitterest tears shed over graves are for words left unsaid and deeds left undone.

Harriet Beecher Stowe

Four times a widow...

Two women were talking, one was upset and the other asked her what the matter was.

"I've been married four times and all my husbands have passed away," she said.

The first woman asked, "What sort of work did they do?"

The widow replied, "My first husband was a millionaire, my second was a magician, the third was a clergyman and the fourth a funeral director."

"Oh," said the first woman, "One for the money, two for the show, three to get ready and four to go...."

> There is a time for everything... a time to be born and a time to die... a time to cry and a time to laugh... a time to grieve and a time to dance.
>
> ***The Bible*, Ecclesiastes 3:1, 2, 4**

BIBLE

A woman who did a lot of travelling for her work always got nervous when on an aeroplane so she always took her Bible along with her to read as it helped relax her.

One time, she was sitting next to a man. When he saw her pull out her Bible, he gave a little chuckle and smirk and went back to what he was doing.

After a while, he turned to her and asked, “You don’t really believe all that stuff in there, do you?”

The woman replied, “Of course I do. It is the Bible.”

He said, “Well, what about that bloke that was swallowed by that whale?”

She replied, “Oh, Jonah. Yes, I believe that, it is in the Bible.”

He asked, “Well, how do you suppose he survived all that time inside a whale?”

The woman said, “Well, I don’t really know. I guess when I get to heaven, I will ask him.”

“What if he isn’t in heaven?” the man asked sarcastically.

“Then you can ask him,” replied the woman.

If a care is too small to be turned into a prayer, it is too small to be made into a burden.
Unknown

It's not the load that breaks you down, it's the way you carry it.
Lena Horne

What do we live for, if it is not to make life less difficult for each other?
George Eliot

Only good things come from God's hands.
He never gives you more than you can bear.
Every burden prepares you for eternity.
Basilea Schlink

C

CAREERS

Any woman who has a career and a family automatically develops something in the way of two personalities, like two sides of a dollar bill, each different in design. But one can complement the other to make a valuable whole. Her problem is to keep the one from draining life from the other.

Ivy Baker Priest, US Treasurer

My daughter just thinks that all mums fly the space shuttle.

Air Force Col. Eileen Collins

Develop your business first before building your house.

***The Bible*, Proverbs 24:27**

When people ask me why I am running as a woman, I always answer, "What choice do I have?"

Pat Schroeder

Defined by your work?

A man in a hot-air balloon realised he was lost. He reduced altitude and spotted a woman below. He descended a bit more and shouted, "Excuse me, can you help me? I promised a friend I would meet him an hour ago, but I don't know where I am."

The woman below replied, "You are in a hot-air balloon, hovering approximately 30 feet above the ground. You are between 40 and 41 degrees north and 59 and 60 degrees west."

"You must be an engineer," said the balloonist.

"I am," said the woman. "How did you know?"

"Well," answered the balloonist, "Everything you told me is technically correct, but I have no idea what to make of your information, and the fact is I am still lost. Frankly, you've not been much help so far."

The woman below responded, "You must be in management."

"I am," said the balloonist. "How did you know?"

"Well," said the woman, "you don't know where you are or where you are going. You have risen to where you are due to a large quantity of hot air. You made a promise which you have no idea how to keep, and you expect people below you to solve your problems. The fact is you are in exactly the same position you were in before we met, but now, somehow, it's my fault."

CHANGE

The challenges of change are always hard. It is important that we begin to unpack those challenges... and realise that we each have a role that requires *us* to change and become more responsible for shaping our own future.

Hillary Rodham Clinton

The fastest way to change society is to mobilise the women of the world.

Charles Malik, former president, United Nations General Assembly

It's not so much that we're afraid of change or so in love with the old ways, but it's that place in between that we fear... It's like being between trapezes. There's nothing to hold on to.

Marilyn Ferguson

I am convinced that the influence of an army of godly women will be incalculable – in our homes, our churches, and our culture. Will you be one of those women?

Nancy Leigh DeMoss

If you don't like the way the world is, you change it. You have an obligation to change it. You just do it one step at a time... You really can change the world if you care enough.

Marian Wright Edelman

Never doubt that a small group of thoughtful, committed citizens can change the world. Indeed, it is the only thing that ever has.

Margaret Mead

CHARACTER

A worthy wife is her husband's joy and crown;
A shameful wife saps his strength.

***The Bible*, Proverbs 12:4**

Character cannot be developed in ease and quiet. Only through experience of trial and suffering can the soul be strengthened, vision cleared, ambition inspired, and success achieved.

Helen Keller

Influence follows close upon the heels of character; and whatever we are, that we shall in the end be acknowledged to be.

Caroline Dall (1852)

A mother's example sketches the outline of her child's character.

Mrs H. O. Ward

One of the best ways to measure people is how they behave when something free is offered.

Ann Landers

The best index to a person's character is (a) how he treats people who can't do him any good, and (b) how he treats people who can't fight back.

Abigail van Buren

Never grow a wishbone, daughter, where your backbone should be.

Clementine Paddleford

Bad company corrupts good character

***The Bible*, 1 Corinthians 15:33**

CHEERFULNESS

I'm not happy, I'm cheerful. There's a difference.
A happy woman has no cares at all.
A cheerful woman has cares
but has learned how to deal with them

Beverly Sills

A glad heart makes a happy face...
and for the happy heart, life is a continual feast.
A cheerful heart is good medicine...

The Bible, Proverbs 15:13, 15; 17:22

You find yourself refreshed in the presence of cheerful people. Why not make an honest effort to confer that pleasure on others? Half the battle is gained if you never allow yourself to say anything gloomy.

Lydia M. Child

CHILDBIRTH

A woman went to her doctor who verified that she was pregnant. This was her first pregnancy.

The doctor asked her if she had any questions.

She replied, "Well, I'm a little worried about the pain. How much will childbirth hurt?"

The doctor answered, "Well, that varies from woman to woman and pregnancy to pregnancy and besides, it's difficult to describe pain."

"I know, but can't you give me some idea?" she asked.

"Grab your upper lip and pull it out a little..."

"Like this?"

"A little more..."

"Like this?"

"No. A little more..."

"Like this?"

"Yes. Does that hurt?"

"A little bit."

"Now stretch it over your head!"

Before you were conceived I wanted you, before you were born I loved you, before you were here an hour I would die for you: This is the miracle of life.

Maureen Hawkins

Death, and taxes and childbirth! There is never a convenient time for any of them.

Margaret Mitchell, *Gone with the Wind*

If men had babies, they would only ever have one each.

Diana, Princess of Wales, *The Observer*, 29 July 1984

CHILDRAISING

To nourish children and raise them against the odds is, in any time, any place, more valuable than to fix bolts in cars or design nuclear weapons.

Marilyn French

Even children are known by the way they act, whether their conduct is pure and right. Teach your children to choose the right path, and when they are older, they will remain on it.

***The Bible*, Proverbs 20:11 & 22:6**

Parents can only give good advice or put children on the right paths, but the final forming of a person's character lies in their own hands.

Anne Frank

I just want my kids to love who they are, have happy lives and find something they want to do and make peace with that. Your job as a parent is to give your kids not only the instincts and talents to survive, but help them enjoy their lives.

Susan Sarandon, *Readers' Digest*, May 2002

Parents who are afraid to put their foot down usually have children who tread on their toes.

Chinese proverb

I looked on childrearing not only as a work of love and duty but as a profession that was fully interesting and challenging as any honourable profession in the world and one that demanded the best that I could bring to it.

Rose Kennedy

Don't make your children angry by the way you treat them. Rather bring them up with the discipline and instruction approved by the Lord... Don't aggravate your children. If you do, they will become discouraged and stop trying.

***The Bible*, Colossians 3:21**

Latin: **Loco parentis**
English: **Children drive their parents crazy.**

The real menace about dealing with a five-year-old is that in no time at all you begin to sound like a five-year-old.

Jean Kerr

CHILDREN

Children keep us in check. Their laughter prevents our hearts from hardening. Their dreams ensure we never lose our drive to make ours a better world. They are the greatest disciplinarians known to mankind.

Queen Rania of Jordan,
Hello Magazine

God sends children to enlarge our hearts,
and make us unselfish
and full of kindly sympathies and affections.

Mary Howitt

Children have the right…
- to affection, love and understanding.
- to adequate nutrition and medical care.
- to free education.
- to full opportunity for play and recreation.
- to a name and a nationality.
- to special care if handicapped.
- to be among the first to receive relief in times of disaster.
- to learn to be a useful member of society and to develop individual abilities.
- to be brought up in a spirit of peace and universal brotherhood.
- to enjoy these rights, regardless of race, colour, sex, religion, national or social origin.

UN Declaration of the Rights of the Child

There are two things that children wear out – their clothes and their parents.

Out of the mouths of children…

After church on the way home, mother asked her small son what they talked about in Sunday school. The little boy told her that they talked about the creation story and how God had taken a rib from Adam's side and made a wife for him. After lunch mother found him doubled over in pain. Mother asks what's wrong. He replies, "My side hurts, Mummy. I think I'm having a wife."

No one knows how children will turn out; a great tree often springs from a tender plant.

Norwegian proverb

Children are the proof we've been here... they are the best thing and the most impossible thing.

Allison Pearson,
I Don't Know How She Does It

Q: What is a house without children?
A: Paid for.

Making the decision to have a child – it's momentous. It is to decide forever to have your heart go walking outside your body.

Elizabeth Stone

The best way to keep children home is to make the home atmosphere pleasant – and let the air out of the tyres.

Dorothy Parker

It is not a bad thing that children should occasionally, and politely, put parents in their place.

Colette

When I was young my parents told me what to do. Now I am old, my children tell me what to do. When will I be able to do what I want?

Anon.

CHOCOLATE

Chocolate is the greatest gift to women ever created...it's something that should be had on a daily basis.
Sandra Bullock

I think I've scratched the surface after 20 years of marriage. Women want chocolate and conversation.
Mel Gibson

The rules of chocolate

If you've got melted chocolate all over your hands, you're eating it too slowly.

Chocolate-covered raisins, cherries, orange slices and strawberries all count as fruit, so eat as many as you want.

The problem: How to get two pounds of chocolate home from the supermarket in a hot car. The solution: Eat it in the car park.

Diet tip: Eat a chocolate bar before each meal. It'll take the edge off your appetite, and you'll eat less.

If I eat equal amounts of dark chocolate and white chocolate, is that a balanced diet? Don't they actually counteract each other?

Chocolate has many preservatives. Preservatives make you look younger. Therefore, you need to eat more chocolate.

Put "eat chocolate" at the top of your list of things to do today. That way, at least you'll get one thing done.

A nice box of chocolates can provide your total daily intake of calories in one place. Now, isn't that handy?

If not for chocolate, there would be no need for tummy-control underwear. An entire garment industry would be devastated. You can't let that happen, can you?

All I need to know about life, I learned from eating chocolate

Some people are semi-sweet, others are just plain nutty.

The best things in life are not fat-free.

You never know a person until you've shared a box of chocolates with them.

An ounce of truffles is worth a pound of anything.

Flowers and champagne may set the stage but it's chocolate that steals the show.

Don't cry over spilled milk, unless it's chocolate milk.

Blind dates are like chocolate – they're usually chunky and they quickly disappear.

Milk chocolate... for all it's worth.

Money can't buy you love – but it can buy you chocolate!

I don't eat it, because otherwise I remember how much I love it, and I'd eat it every day.

Jodie Foster

Did you know that…?

Chocolate isn't so bad for you after all:

Dark chocolate has much less caffeine than a cup of coffee. A bar of dark chocolate has only 10–30 mgs of caffeine compared to 100 mgs in a cup of coffee!

The ability of the sugar in chocolate to drive up blood sugar (glycaemia index) is about the same as oatmeal.

Chocolate is rich in cell-protecting antioxidants. Dark chocolate has twice as much as milk chocolate, and white chocolate has NONE! So avoid white chocolate unless you are a messy eater!

CHOICE

The individual woman is required…a thousand times a day to choose either to accept her appointed role and thereby rescue her good disposition out of the wreckage of her self-respect, or else follow an independent line of behaviour and rescue her self-respect out of the wreckage of her good disposition.

Jeanette Rankin

Lisa Gordon, 38, the youngest woman director of a British publicly-listed company, recently quit her job to spend more time with her children. She is quoted as having said: "Women can have it all; I am just choosing not to want it all."

I discovered I always have choices and sometimes it's only a choice of attitude.

Judith M. Knowlton

I believe that we are solely responsible for our choices, and we have to accept the consequences of every deed, word and thought throughout our lifetime.

Elisabeth Kübler-Ross

If you have to make a choice, you do have to take responsibility for what is given up, rather than blame others for what is denied.

Nigella Lawson, *Daily Telegraph*

We need to teach the next generation of children from Day One that they are responsible for their lives. Mankind's greatest gift, also its greatest curse, is that we have free choice. We can make our choices built from love or from fear.

Elisabeth Kübler-Ross

That guy just cut right in front of me. But I'm not going to let it bother me. No. I'm on my way to work and I decided it doesn't matter who wants to cut in front of my lane today. I'm not going to let it bother me one bit. Once I get to work and find myself a parking space, if somebody wants to jump ahead of me and take it, I'm going to let them.

Oprah Winfrey

Female reindeer

According to the Alaska Department of Fish and Game, while both male and female reindeer grow antlers in the summer each year, male reindeer drop their antlers at the beginning of winter, usually late November to mid-December.

Female reindeer retain their antlers till after they give birth in the spring. Therefore, according to every historical rendition depicting Santa's reindeer, every single one of them, from Rudolph to Blitzen, had to be a female.

We should've known.

Only women would be able to drag a fat man in a red velvet suit all around the world in one night and not get lost....

A five-year-old girl was watching as the nativity scene was set up for the carol service. She was mesmerised by all the figurines – especially the baby Jesus. When she asked what the manger was, her teacher explained that they didn't have a crib for Jesus, so they had to lay a blanket on the hay and put him there. She thought about that for a minute, and then asked, "Did they have to use a manger for his car seat, too?"

’Twas the Night Before Christmas…for mums

’Twas the night before Christmas,
when all through the abode
Only one creature was stirring – she
was cleaning the commode.
The children were sleeping all snug in
their beds,
while visions of *Lego* and *Barbie* flipped
through their heads.
The dad was snoring in front of a
droning TV,
With a half-built bicycle propped on his
knee.
So only Mum heard the reindeer
hooves clatter,
Which made her sigh, “Now what is the
matter?”
With the toilet bowl brush still
clutched in her hand,
She descended the stairs and saw the
old man.
He was covered with ashes and soot,
which fell with a shrug,
“Oh, great,” muttered Mum, “now I
must clean the rug.”
“Ho! Ho! Ho!” cried Santa, “I’m glad
you’re awake,
your gift was especially difficult to
make.”
“Thanks, Santa,” she said, “all I want is
time alone.”
“Exactly!” he chuckled, “So, I’ve made
you a clone.”
“A clone?” she muttered, “What good
is that?”
“Run along, Santa, I’ve no time for chit
chat.”
Then out walked the clone – the
mother’s twin;
Same hair, same eyes, same double
chin.
“She’ll cook, she’ll dust, and she’ll mop
every mess.
You’ll relax, take it easy, now you can
work less.”
“Fantastic!” Mum cheered. “My dream
has come true!
I’ll shop, I’ll read, and I’ll sleep a night
through!”
From the room upstairs, the youngest
did fret.
“Mummy! Come quickly, I’m scared and
I’m wet.”
The clone replied, “I’m coming,
sweetheart.”
“Hey,” the mum smiled, “she sure
knows her part.”
The clone changed the small one and
hummed her a tune,
as she bundled the child in a blanket
cocoon.
“You’re the best mummy ever. I really
love you.”
The clone smiled and sighed, “And I
love you, too.”
The mum frowned and said, “Sorry,
Santa, no deal.
That’s my child’s love she is trying to
steal.”
Smiling wisely, Santa said, “To me it is
clear,
Only one loving mother is needed
here.”
The mum kissed her child and tucked
her in bed.
“Thank you, Santa, for clearing my
head.
I sometimes forget, it won’t be very
long,
when they’ll be too old for my cradle
and song.”
The clock on the mantel began to
chime.
Santa whispered to the clone, “It works
every time.”
With the clone by his side, Santa said,
“Good night.
Merry Christmas, dear Mum, you’ll be
all right.”

Author unknown

CIRCUMSTANCES

Whatever your lot in life... build something on it.

Anon.

People are always blaming their circumstances for what they are. I don't believe in circumstances. The people who get on in this world are the people who get up and look for the circumstances they want, and, if they can't find them, they make them.

George Bernard Shaw

I have learned how to get along happily whether I have much or little. I know how to live on almost nothing or with everything. I have learned the secret of living in every situation, whether it is with a full stomach or empty, with plenty or little. For I can do everything with the help of Christ who gives me the strength I need.

St Paul, *The Bible*, Philippians 4:11–13

CLOTHING

Of all things you wear, your expression is the most important.

Anon.

I base most of my fashion taste on what doesn't itch.

Gilda Radner

And why worry about your clothes? Look at the lilies and how they grow. They don't work or make their clothing, yet Solomon in all his glory was not dressed as beautifully as they are.

Jesus Christ, *The Bible*, Matthew 6:28–29

Many a woman who thinks she has purchased a dress for a ridiculous price has actually bought it for an absurd figure.

Anon.

A wife remarked to her husband after the church service: "Did you see the hat Mrs Jones was wearing?" "No," said her husband, "I didn't." "Did you see the new dress Mrs Smith had on?" she asked. "I'm afraid I didn't," said her husband. To this his wife replied: "Well a lot of good it does *you* to go to church!"

You just want to look casual and cute, and not have everything on display.

Jennifer Lopez, *In Style*

Did you know that...?

Fashion advisors advocate that the more you intend to spend on an item of clothing, the more classic the style you ought to choose.

Fashion is an expression of the person wearing the clothes. It has nothing to do with age, and everything to do with fun…when people accuse me now of being mutton dressed as lamb, I couldn't care less.

Zandra Rhodes,
***Daily Express*, 2 June 2003**

CLUTTER

A clear house is a clear mind.

Be ruthless about throwing out unwanted things.

Sheila Teague,
***Good Housekeeping*,**
June 2003

A lot of people buy things they don't need, with money they don't have, to impress people they don't even like.

J. John

One person's mess is merely another person's filing system.

Margo Kaufman

There is a time to keep and a time to throw away.

***The Bible*, Ecclesiastes 3:6**

A place for everything, and everything in its place.

Mrs Beeton, *Book of Household Management*

Obsessive clutter is often a symptom of underlying emotional issues. Letting go of your junk is the best way of taking the first step towards recovery and confronting the real issues that cause you to hold on to things.

Dawna Walter and Mark Franks, *How to De-junk your Life*, BBC Worldwide Ltd (2002)

COMMITMENT

Whatever our souls are made of, his and mine are the same…

Emily Brontë, *Wuthering Heights*

Never reach out your hand unless you're willing to extend an arm.

Elizabeth Fuller

If the grass looks greener on the other side of the fence, it's because they take care of it.

Source unknown

I will go wherever you go
And live wherever you live;
Your people will be my people,
Your God will be my God.
I will die where you die
And be buried there.
May the Lord punish me severely
if I allow anything but death to separate us!
The Bible, Ruth 1:16–17

What greater thing is there for two human souls than to feel that they are joined for life – to strengthen each other in all labour, to rest on each other in all sorrow, to minister to each other in all pain, to be one with each other in silent, unspeakable memories at the moment of the last parting?
George Eliot

COMMON SENSE

Common sense is the knack of seeing things as they are, and doing things as they ought to be done.
Harriet Beecher Stowe

It is a thousand times better to have common sense without education than to have education without common sense.
Robert Green Ingersoll

People change and forget to tell each other.

Lillian Hellman

Good communication is as stimulating as black coffee, and just as hard to sleep after.

Anne Morrow Lindbergh

Did you know that... ?

On average a wife will say she needs to spend 45–60 minutes a day in meaningful conversation with her husband, and the husband will say he needs 15–20 minutes once or twice a week.

One of the basic causes for all the trouble in the world today is that people talk too much and think too little. They act impulsively without thinking. I always try to think before I talk.

Margaret Chase Smith

Before speaking:

T – is it true?
H – is it helpful?
I – is it inspiring?
N – is it necessary?
K – is it kind?

When we have the courage to speak out – to break our silence – we inspire the rest of the "moderates" in our communities to speak up and voice their views.

Sharon Schuster

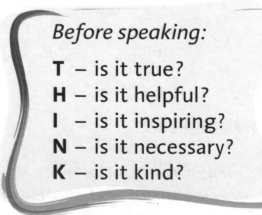

Self-expression must pass into communication for its fulfilment.

Pearl S. Buck

COMPLIMENTS

When it comes to compliments, women are ravenous, blood-sucking monsters – all they want is more, more, more!

Homer Simpson

COMPROMISE

Don't compromise yourself. You are all you've got.

Janis Joplin

If you just set out to be liked, you would be prepared to compromise on anything at any time, and you would achieve nothing.

Margaret Thatcher

Most people hew the battlements of life from compromise, erecting their impregnable keeps from judicious submissions, fabricating their philosophical drawbridges from emotional retractions and scalding marauders in the boiling oil of sour grapes.

Zelda Fitzgerald, *Save Me the Waltz* (1932)

CONDUCT

Well-behaved women rarely make history.
Laurel Thatcher Ulrich

A wise woman builds her house; a foolish woman tears hers down with her own hands.
***The Bible*, Proverbs 14:1**

CONSCIENCE

Conscience that isn't hitched up to common sense is a mighty dangerous thing.
Margaret Deland,
The Promises of Alice

While conscience is our friend, all is at peace; however once it is offended, farewell to a tranquil mind.
Lady Mary Wortley Montagu

Conscience is the internal perception of the rejection of a particular wish operating within us.
Sigmund Freud, *Totem and Taboo*

I cannot and will not cut my conscience to fit this year's fashions.
Lillian Hellman

CONTRACEPTION

My best birth control now is just to leave the lights on.

Joan Rivers

The most effective form of birth control I know is spending the day with my kids.

Jill Bensley

An American woman who spread contraceptive jelly on her toast every morning is suing her chemist after becoming pregnant. Lawyers representing the woman, who thought the jelly was edible, are claiming £300,000 for the "inconvenience".

***The Week*, 21 June 2003**

Did you know that… ?

Figures from the Office of National Statistics show that in a study of women born between 1954 and 1958, graduates, who entered the work place at the end of the 1960s, were 50% less likely to have children than non-graduates. 22.5% of graduates remained childless compared to 15% of non-graduates.

Sociologists believe these figures reflect the expectations of an era prior to the Sexual Discrimination Act, in which a career and motherhood didn't mix.

She who will ever taste and try, will burn her fingers in the pie.
Norwegian proverb

My husband has a great way of keeping pans sparkling clean – he never uses them!
Anon.

Life is too short to stuff a mushroom.
Shirley Conran, *Superwoman* (1975)

When it comes to butter versus margarine, I trust cows more than I trust chemists.
Joan Gussow

DINNER IS READY WHEN THE SMOKE ALARM GOES OFF.

Ideal way vs. real women's way

Ideal way 1
Stuff a miniature marshmallow in the bottom of a sugar cone to prevent ice cream drips.

The real women's way
Just suck the ice cream out of the bottom of the cone, for goodness' sake. You are probably lying on the couch with your feet up eating it anyway.

Ideal way 2
To keep potatoes from budding, place an apple in the bag with the potatoes.

The real women's way
Buy instant mashed potato mix and keep it in the pantry for up to a year.

Ideal way 3
When a cake recipe calls for flouring the baking tin, use a bit of the dry cake mix instead and there won't be any white mess on the outside of the cake.

The real women's way
Supermarkets sell cakes. They even do decorated versions.

Ideal way 4
If you accidentally over-salt a dish while it's still cooking, drop in a potato slice.

The real women's way
If you over-salt a dish while you are cooking, that's tough. Please recite with me the real women's motto: "I made it and you will eat it and I don't care how bad it tastes."

Ideal way 5
Wrap celery in aluminium foil when putting it in the refrigerator and it will keep for weeks.

The real women's way
It could keep for ever. Who eats it?

Ideal way 6
Brush some beaten egg white over piecrust before baking to yield a beautiful glossy finish.

The real women's way
The frozen pie directions don't include brushing any egg white over the crust so I don't do that.

Ideal way 7
Cure for headaches: Take a lime, cut it in half and rub it on your forehead. The throbbing will go away.

The real women's way
Cure for headaches: Take a lime, cut it in half and drop it in a shot of tequila. Drink the tequila. You might still have the headache, but who cares?

Ideal way 8
If you have a problem opening jars, try using latex dishwashing gloves. They give a non-slip grip that makes opening jars easy.

The real women's way
What's the point of blokes then?

And finally the most important tip – ideal way 9
Freeze leftover wine into ice cubes for future use in casseroles and sauces.

The real women's way
Leftover wine? Hello!

No one should be excused from kitchen duty except for sickness or because they are more usefully engaged elsewhere, because, through this service, the reward of an increase in charity is gained.

The Rule of St Benedict

Did you know that… ?
It takes two litres of water to cook macaroni for a family, and another two litres of water to wash the pot.

Too many cooks spoil the broth and too many brews spoil the cook.

Anon.

Ham for dinner

A young woman was preparing a ham dinner. After she cut off the end of the ham, she placed the ham in a pan for baking.

Her friend asked her, "Why did you cut off the end of the ham?"

She replied, "I really don't know, but my mother always did, so I thought you were supposed to."

Later, when talking to her mother, she asked her why she cut off the end of the ham before baking it, and her mother replied, "I really don't know, but that's the way my mum always did it."

A few weeks later while visiting her grandmother, the young woman asked, "Grandma, why is it that you cut off the end of a ham before you bake it?"

Her grandmother replied, "Well, dear, it would never fit into my baking pan."

COURAGE

Courage is fear that has said its prayers.

Anon.

Courage is the atom of change.

Bettina R. Flores

Courage, it would seem, is nothing less than the power to overcome danger, misfortune, fear, injustice, while continuing to affirm inwardly that life with all its sorrows is good; that everything is meaningful even if in a sense beyond our understanding; and that there is always a tomorrow.

Dorothy Thompson

Courage is what it takes to stand up and speak;
Courage is also what it takes to sit down and listen.

Anon.

Have courage for the great sorrows of life, and patience for the small ones. And when you have laboriously accomplished your daily task, go to sleep in peace. God is awake.

Victor Hugo

Courage is reclaiming your life after a devastating event robs you of your confidence and self-esteem. It is facing tomorrow with a firm resolve to reach deep within yourself to find another strength, another talent… It is taking yourself to another level of your own existence where you are once again whole, productive, special.

Catherine Britton

CRITICISM

It is better to be criticised by a wise person than to be praised by a fool.

***The Bible*, Ecclesiastes 7:5**

Before you criticise someone,
walk a mile in her shoes.
That way, if she gets angry, she'll
be a mile away – and barefoot.

Sarah Jackson

Did you know that… ?

It is thought to be a masculine trait to view criticism as constructive advice, to be grateful for it and act on it. It is a feminine trait, however, to see criticism as an attack, viewing every interaction as personal and condescending.

CRYING

Did you know that…?
A woman cries on average five times more often than a man.

CURIOSITY

When curiosity turns to serious matters, it's called research.

Marie von Ebner-Eschenbach, *Aphorisms*

The cure for boredom is curiosity.
There is no cure for curiosity.

Ellen Parr

Be less curious about people and more curious about ideas.

Marie Curie

D

DAUGHTERS

There is a point where you aren't as much mum and daughter as you are adults and friends. It doesn't happen for everyone – but it did for Mum and me.

Jamie Lee Curtis

DEATH

Don't be afraid your life will end;
be afraid that it will never begin.

Grace Hansen

I don't want to get to the end of my life and find that I have just lived the length of it. I want to have lived the width of it as well.

Diane Ackerman

Death is the opening of a more subtle life. In the flower, it sets free the perfume; in the chrysalis, the butterfly; in man, the soul.

Juliette Adam

Epitaph of a housewife

Here lies a woman, who was always tired,
She lived in a house where help wasn't hired.
Her last words on earth were, "Friends, I am going
Where there's no washing, ironing or sewing;
To a place where all is to my wishes,
No meals to cook and no washing of dishes.
Don't mourn for me now; don't mourn for me ever –
'cos I'm going to do nothing for ever and ever."

Anon.

In the last analysis, it is our conception of death which decides our answers to all the questions that life puts to us.

Dag Hammarskjöld

Because I have loved life, I shall have no sorrow to die.

Amelia Burr

You don't get to choose how
you're going to die.
Or when.
But you can decide how
you're going to live now.

Joan Baez

A little girl said, "Grandpa, can I sit on your lap?"

"Of course you can," her grandfather replied.

As she sat on his lap she said, "Grandpa, can you make a sound like a frog?"

"A sound like a frog? Well, I'm sure I can make a sound like a frog."

The girl said, "Grandpa, will you please, please make a sound like a frog?"

Perplexed, her grandfather asked, "Sweetheart, why do you want me to make a sound like a frog?"

The little girl replied, " 'Cause Grandma said that when you croak, we're going to Florida!"

DECISIONS

An inadvertent decision

There were three people hanging on to a rope that came down from a helicopter. There were two men and one woman. They all decided that one person should get off because if they did not, the rope would break and everyone would die. No one could decide who should go. So finally the woman gave a really touching speech, saying how she would give up her life to save the others, because women were used to giving up things for their husbands and children, and not receiving anything in return.

When she finished speaking, both men clapped.

Decisions, decisions

Julie found that her difficulty in making even the simplest decisions was causing her problems at work. Finally she decided to seek professional help.

"Tell me, Julie," said the psychologist, "I understand you have trouble making decisions."

Julie's brow furrowed. "Well," she said, "Yes…and no."

DEFEAT

The price of giving up is always wondering what could have been.

Anon.

Whoever said anybody has a right to give up?

Marian Wright Edelman

Being defeated is often a temporary condition, Giving up is what makes it permanent.

Marilyn Mach Vos Savant

DEPRESSION

Singing cheerful songs to a person whose heart is heavy is as bad as stealing someone's jacket in cold weather or rubbing salt in a wound.

***The Bible*, Proverbs 25:20**

So often we are depressed by what remains to be done and forget to be thankful for all that has been done.

Marian Wright Edelman

DETERMINATION

The baby rises to its feet, takes a step, is overcome with triumph and joy – and falls flat on its face. It is a pattern for all that is to come! But learn from the bewildered baby. Lurch to your feet again. You'll make the sofa in the end.

Pam Brown

DIETING

I'm on a sea food diet...
All the food I see, I eat!

Anon.

I went on a fourteen-day diet...and all I lost was two weeks.

Have your cake and eat it

A woman in our diet club was lamenting that she had gained weight.

She'd made her family's favourite cake over the weekend, she reported, and they'd eaten half of it at dinner.

The next day, she said, she kept staring at the other half, until finally she cut a thin slice for herself. One slice led to another, and soon the whole cake was gone.

The woman went on to tell us how upset she was with her lack of willpower, and how she knew her husband would be disappointed.

Everyone commiserated; until someone asked what her husband said when he found out.

She smiled. "He never found out. I made another cake and ate half!"

"Rules" of dieting

If you drink a diet drink with a chocolate bar, the calories in the chocolate bar are cancelled out by the diet drink.

When you eat with someone else, calories don't count if they eat more than you do.

Calories in food used for medicinal purposes *never* count. Examples: hot chocolate or ice cream.

If you fatten everyone else around you, then you look thinner.

Movie-related foods such as pick 'n' mix and popcorn do not have additional calories because everyone knows that movies aren't real.

When preparing food, things licked off spoons and knives have no calories. Examples: peanut butter on a knife when making a child's sandwich and chocolate cake mix for contribution to school cake stall.

Broken chocolate biscuit pieces contain no fat. It leaks out.

Foods that are the same colour have the same number of calories. e.g: Spinach and pistachio ice cream; mushrooms and white chocolate.

Calories are a unit of heat. Therefore, frozen foods have no calories. Examples include ice cream, frozen pies and solid chicken nuggets.

Food eaten standing up doesn't count to your daily calorie allowance.

We have little choice about being part of a culture in which youth is celebrated over age, and thin is celebrated over well-rounded. But we do have a choice about whether to live in the challenge of the gospel that tells us we are completely loved as we are, or whether to believe what the airbrush is saying.

Jo Ind, *Fat is a Spiritual Issue*

Desperation is a woman plucking her eyebrows before she steps on the scales.

Losing weight

A woman was terribly overweight, so her doctor put her on a diet.

He told her, “I want you to eat regularly for two days, then skip a day, eat regularly for two days, then skip a day. Repeat this procedure for two weeks. The next time I see you, you’ll have lost at least five pounds.”

When the woman returned, she shocked the doctor. She had lost nearly 20 pounds.

“Why, that’s amazing!” the doctor said. “Did you follow my instructions?”

The woman nodded. “I’ll tell you though; I thought I was going to drop dead that third day.”

“From hunger, you mean?” asked the doctor.

“No, from all that skipping!”

DIFFERENCE

The human species is divided into two genders which ensure its production and reproduction. To wish to get rid of sexual difference is to call for a genocide more radical than any form of destruction there has ever been in history.
Luce Irigaray, *Je, Tu, Nous – towards a culture of difference*

Whether women are better than men I cannot say – but I can say that they are certainly no worse.
Golda Meir

Greetings, I am pleased to see that we are different. May we together become greater than the sum of us.
Vulcan greeting

Post-feminism seeks to embrace difference and not to erase it. It recognises that there are intrinsic psychological and biological differences between men and women ... the problem is what to make of these differences. This should not bar women from certain jobs, or from access to political power.
Kevin O'Donnell, *A History of Ideas*, Lion (2003)

DIVORCE

To get divorced because love has died is like selling your car because it's run out of petrol.
Diane Sollee, smartmarriages.com

I think if you walk out of a marriage because it's had a down and expect a new love or a new marriage to be only up, you're in for a rude awakening.
Mary Archer, *Radio Times*, 17–23 May 2003

A judge was interviewing a woman regarding her pending divorce, and asked, "What are the grounds for your divorce?"

She replied, "About four acres and a nice little home in the middle of the property with a stream running by."

"No," he said, "I mean what is the foundation of this case?"

"It is made of concrete, brick and mortar," she responded.

"I mean," he continued, "What are your relations like?"

"I have an aunt and uncle living here in town, and so do my husband's parents."

He said, "Do you have a real grudge?"

"No," she replied, "We have a two-car carport and have never really needed one."

"Please," he tried again, "is there any infidelity in your marriage?"

"Yes, both my son and daughter have stereo sets. We don't necessarily like the music, but the answer to your questions is yes."

"Ma'am, does your husband ever beat you up?"

"Yes," she responded, "about twice a week, he gets up earlier than I do."

Finally, in frustration, the judge asked, "Lady, why do you want a divorce?"

"Oh, I don't want a divorce," she replied. "I've never wanted a divorce. My husband does. He said he can't communicate with me."

Did you know that…?

In 2001 the most frequent fact on which divorce was granted to a woman in England and Wales was the unreasonable behaviour of her husband, while for a man, it was separation for two years with consent.

And you wonder "why" it didn't last

She married him because he was such a "strong man".
She divorced him because he was such a "dominating male".

He married her because she was so "fragile and cute".
He divorced her because she was so "weak and helpless".

She married him because "he is a good provider".
She divorced him because "all he thinks about is business".

He married her because "she reminds me of my mother".
He divorced her because "she's getting more like her mother every day".

She married him because he was "happy and romantic".
She divorced him because he was "shiftless and fun-loving".

He married her because she was "steady and sensible".
He divorced her because she was "boring and dull".

She married him because he was "the life of the party".
She divorced him because "he's a party boy".

Source unknown

My daughter is thinking of becoming a doctor – she has the handwriting for it.

Never go to a doctor whose office plants have died.

Erma Bombeck

Shock treatment

A woman went to the doctor's surgery where she was seen by one of the new doctors, but after about four minutes in the examination room, she burst out, screaming as she ran down the corridor. An older doctor stopped her and asked what the problem was, and she told him her story. After listening, he made her sit down and told her to go and relax in another room. The older doctor marched down the corridor back to where the first doctor was and demanded, "What's the matter with you? Mrs Smith is 63 years old, she has four grown-up children and seven grandchildren, and you told her she was pregnant?" The new doctor continued to write on his clipboard and, without looking up, said, "Does she still have the hiccups?"

Goals are dreams with deadlines.
Diana Scharf Hunt

Before your dreams can come true, you have to have those dreams.
Dr Joyce Brothers

Within our dreams and aspirations we find our opportunities.
Sue Ebaugh

Without leaps of imagination, or dreaming, we lose the excitement of possibilities. Dreaming, after all, is a form of planning.
Gloria Steinem

Don't be afraid of the space between your dreams and reality. If you can dream it, you can make it so.
Belva Davis

If your dreams turn to dust...vacuum!
Source unknown

To make your dreams come true...you have to stay awake.

Some people see things as they are and ask "Why?" Other people dream things as they could be and ask, "Why not?"
Anon.

You can't just sit there and wait for people to give you that golden dream; you've got to get out there and make it happen for yourself.
Diana Ross

Dreaming all the time instead of working is foolishness.
***The Bible*, Ecclesiastes 5:7**

DRINK

One reason I don't drink is because I wish to know when I am having a good time.

Nancy Astor

DRIVING

The speeding ticket

"What am I supposed to do with this?" grumbled the woman motorist as the policeman handed her a speeding ticket.

"Keep it," the policeman said. "When you collect four of them you get a bicycle."

The one thing that unites all human beings, regardless of age, gender, religion, economic status or ethnic background, is that, deep down inside, we *all* believe that we are above-average drivers.

D. Barry

EDUCATION

Thank goodness I was never sent to school; it would have rubbed off some of the originality.

Beatrix Potter

No book has yet been written in praise of a woman who let her husband and children starve or suffer while she invented even the most useful things, or wrote books, or expressed herself in art, or evolved philosophic systems.

Anna Garlin Spencer, *Woman's Share in Social Culture*, 1912

Education is for improving the lives of others and for leaving your community and world better than you found it.

Marian Wright Edelman

I will not weary myself with seeking beyond what God wants me to know. Instead I will abide in peace with the understanding God has given me, and I will let this occupy my mind. If we are to see properly, we must pluck out of our eyes our own presumption. If we gaze too long at the sun, we go blind; in this manner, I think, does pride blind many of us who want to know too much.

Catherine of Genoa (1447–1510), *Life and Teachings*

...the wit of a man or a woman waxeth dull and unapt to do or understand anything perfectly, unless it always be occupied upon some manner of study.

Elizabeth Tudor (1544)

We have a hunger of the mind which asks for knowledge of all around us, and the more we gain, the more is our desire; the more we see, the more we are capable of seeing.

Maria Mitchell

The human mind prefers to be spoon-fed with the thoughts of others, but deprived of such nourishment it will, reluctantly, begin to think for itself – and such thinking, remember, is original thinking and may have valuable results.

Agatha Christie

To repeat what others have said, requires education, to challenge it, requires brains.

Mary Pettibone Poole

The joy of learning is as indispensable in study as breathing is in running. Where it is lacking there are no real students, but only poor caricatures of apprentices who, at the end of their apprenticeship, will not even have a trade.

Simone Weil

You must learn day by day, year by year, to broaden your horizon. The more things you love, the more you are interested in, the more you enjoy, the more you are indignant about, the more you have left when anything happens.

Ethel Barrymore

Establishing lasting peace is the work of education; all politics can do is keep us out of war.

Maria Montessori

EFFORT

Do the best you can, where you are, with what you have.

Anon.

Every accomplishment starts with the decision to try.

Anon.

Aspire to be, and all that we are not God will give us credit for trying.

Nannie Burroughs

Work hard and cheerfully at whatever you do, as though you were working for the Lord rather than for people.

***The Bible*, Colossians 3:23**

EMPOWERMENT

Women will not become more empowered merely because we want them to be, but through legislative changes, increased information, and redirection of resources. It would be fatal to overlook this issue.

Gro Harlem Brundtland, Director General, World Health Organization (July 1998 – present), Prime Minister of Norway (1981, 1986–89, 1991–96)

ENGAGEMENT

A young woman brought her fiancé home to meet her parents. After dinner, her mother told her father to find out about the young man. The father invited the fiancé to his study for a conversation.

"So what are your plans?" the father asked the young man.

"I want to study theology," he replied.

"Hmmm," the father said. "Admirable, but how will you provide a nice house for my daughter to live in, as she's accustomed to?"

"I will study," the young man replied, "and God will provide for us."

"And how will you buy her a beautiful engagement ring, such as she deserves?" asked the father.

"I will concentrate on my studies," the young man replied. "God will provide for us."

"And children?" asked the father. "How will you support children?"

"Don't worry, sir, God will provide," replied the fiancé.

The conversation proceeded like this, and each time the father questioned him, the young idealist insisted that God would provide.

Later, the mother asked, "How did it go?"

The father answered, "He has no job and no plans, but the good news is he thinks I'm God."

He that would the daughter win,
Must with the mother first begin.
Old English proverb

We've got a generation now who were born with semi-equality. They don't know how it was before, so they think, this isn't too bad. We're working. We have our attaché cases and our three-piece suits. I get very disgusted with the younger generation of women. We had a torch to pass, and they are just sitting there. They don't realise it can be taken away. Things are going to have to get worse before they join in fighting the battle.

Erma Bombeck

Would men but generously snap our chains, and be content with rational fellowship instead of slavish obedience, they would find us more observant daughters, more affectionate sisters, more faithful wives, more reasonable mothers – in a word, better citizens.

Mary Wollstonecraft

ETERNITY

God exists in eternity. The only point where eternity meets time is in the present. The present is the only time there is.

Marianne Williamson

God has planted eternity in the human heart, but even so, people cannot see the whole scope of God's work from beginning to end.

***The Bible*, Ecclesiastes 3:11**

EXAMPLE

Children have never been too good at listening to their elders, but they have never failed to imitate them.

Anon.

If you as parents cut corners, your children will too. If you lie, they will too. If you spend all your money on yourselves and tithe no portion of it for charities, colleges, churches, synagogues, and civic causes, your children won't either. And if parents snigger at racial and gender jokes, another generation will pass on the poison adults still have not had the courage to snuff out.

Marian Wright Edelman

When you thought I wasn't looking

A message every adult should read, because children are watching you and doing as you do, not as you say.

When you thought I wasn't looking, I saw you hang my first painting on the refrigerator, and I immediately wanted to paint another one.

When you thought I wasn't looking, I saw you feed a stray cat, and I learned that it was good to be kind to animals.

When you thought I wasn't looking, I saw you make my favourite cake for me and I learned that the little things can be the special things in life.

When you thought I wasn't looking, I heard you say a prayer, and I knew there is a God I could always talk to and I learned to trust in God.

When you thought I wasn't looking, I saw you make a meal and take it to a friend who was sick, and I learned that we all have to help take care of each other.

When you thought I wasn't looking, I saw you give of your time and money to help people who had nothing and I learned that those who have something should give to those who don't.

When you thought I wasn't looking, I saw you take care of our house and everyone in it and I learned we have to take care of what we are given.

When you thought I wasn't looking, I saw how you handled your responsibilities, even when you didn't feel good, and I learned that I would have to be responsible when I grow up.

When you thought I wasn't looking, I saw tears come from your eyes and I learned that sometimes things hurt, but it's all right to cry.

When you thought I wasn't looking, I saw that you cared and I wanted to be everything that I could be.

When you thought I wasn't looking, I learned most of life's lessons that I need to know to be a good and productive person when I grow up.

When you thought I wasn't looking, I looked at you and wanted to say, "Thanks for all the things I saw when you thought I wasn't looking."

**There are two ways of spreading light:
to be a candle, or the mirror that reflects it.**
Edith Wharton

Setting an example is not the main means of influencing others – it is the only means.
Anon.

The best gift we can bestow on others is a good example.

EXCELLENCE

Excellence is simply doing the best with what you have, regardless of whether it is cooking a meal, loving our spouse, or working at a job.... Half-heartedness will not only defraud those around oneself but will slowly shrink the boundaries of one's own life as well.
Phil Baker, *Letters to a Lady*

Excellence is not an act but a habit. The things you do the most are the things you will do best.
Marva Collins, "Marva Collins: Teaching Success in the City", *Message*

New daily exercise programme for women:

Every woman should be able to fulfil the following exercise programme without much practice; you probably do most of the exercises already. Some are more beneficial than others... pick and choose your favourites for an exhausting daily workout!

Get up with the lark
Beat around the bush
Jump to conclusions
Climb the walls
Swallow your pride
Pass the buck
Throw your weight around
Drag your heels
Push your luck
Make mountains out of molehills
Hit the nail on the head
Wade through paperwork
Bend over backwards
Jump on the bandwagon
Balance the books
Run around in circles
Blow your own horn
Climb the ladder of success
Pull out the stops
Add fuel to the fire
Open a can of worms
Put your foot in your mouth
Start the ball rolling
Go over the edge
Pick up the pieces
Collapse in a heap.

EXPECTATIONS

Women have always to negotiate a set of more inherently conflicting expectations than men.

David Reason, "Given the choice, why bother with children?" *Church Times*, 9th May 2003

I can't imagine going on when there are no more expectations.

Dame Edith Evans

To free us from the expectations of others, to give us back to ourselves – there lies the great singular power of self-respect.

Joan Didion

Expect nothing, live frugally on surprise.

Alice Walker

Limited expectations yield only limited results.

Susan Laurson Willig

Life is so constructed that an event does not, cannot, will not, match the expectation.

Charlotte Brontë

Cultural expectations shade and colour the images that parents-to-be form. The baby-product ads, showing a woman serenely holding her child, looking blissfully and mysteriously contented, or the television parents, wisely and humorously solving problems....

Ellen Galinsky

EXPERIENCE

Every experience God gives us, every person he puts in our lives, is the perfect preparation for the future that only he can see.

Corrie ten Boom

If you have made mistakes, even serious ones, there is always another chance for you. What we call failure is not the falling down, but the staying down.

Mary Pickford (1893–1979)

Experience is often what you get when you were expecting something else.

Anon.

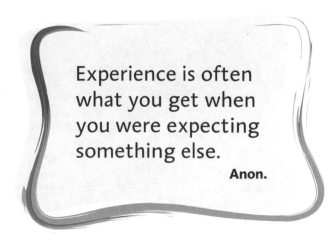

Experience is a hard teacher... it tests first and teaches after.

Anon.

If we could sell our experiences for what they cost us, we'd all be millionairesses.

Abigail Van Buren

Experience is the best teacher. Everyone gets individual instruction.

Anon.

Experience is a revelation in the light of which we renounce our errors of youth for those of age.

Ambrose (Gwinnett) Bierce

Experience isn't interesting till it begins to repeat itself – in fact, till it does that, it hardly is experience.

Elizabeth E. Bowen

Experience is a good teacher, but she sends in terrific bills.

Minna Antrim, *Naked Truth and Veiled Allusions*, 1902

FAILURE

You must accept that you might fail; then, if you do your best and still don't win, at least you can be satisfied that you've tried. If you don't accept failure as a possibility, you don't set high goals and you don't branch out, you don't try – you don't take the risk.

Rosalynn Carter

Failure is another stepping stone to greatness.

Oprah Winfrey

The glory is not in never falling, but in rising every time you fall.

Chinese proverb

If you sometimes fall... do not cease striving to make progress from it, for even out of your fall God will bring some good... Sometimes God allows us to fall in order to reveal to us our sinfulness.

Teresa of Avila, *The Interior Castle*

FAITH

One needs something to believe in, something for which one can have whole-hearted enthusiasm. One needs to feel that one's life has meaning, that one is needed in this world.
Hannah Senesh

Faith is the first factor in a life devoted to service.
Without it, nothing is possible.
With it, nothing is impossible.
Mary McLeod Bethune

Obedience is the fruit of faith;
Patience is the bloom on the fruit.
Christina Rossetti

To believe with certainty, we must begin with doubting.
Polish proverb

Faith is not belief. Belief is passive. Faith is active.
Edith Hamilton, *Witness to the Truth*

Faith is like radar that sees in the fog – the reality of things at a distance that the human eye cannot see.
Corrie ten Boom

What is faith?
It is the confident assurance that what we hope for is going to happen. It is the evidence of things we cannot yet see.
***The Bible*, Hebrews 11:1**

I believe in the light,
even when the sun doesn't shine.
I believe in love,
even when it isn't given.
I believe in God,
even when his voice is silent.

(Found scratched on an air-raid shelter wall in Germany during World War II.)

Faith sees the invisible, believes the unbelievable, and receives the impossible.

Corrie ten Boom

FAMILY LIFE

One of the oldest human needs is having someone wonder when you are coming home at night.

Margaret Mead

If you have never been hated by your child, then you have never been a parent.

Bette Davis

There can be no situation in life in which the conversation of my dear sister will not administer some comfort to me.

Lady Mary Wortley Montagu

The greatest thing in family life is to take a hint when a hint is intended – and not take a hint when a hint isn't intended.

Robert Frost

For the second time in a row, I was forced to impose on the woman with whom I shared a lift to our children's football practices. I phoned and explained that my husband had the car again, so I wouldn't be able to take my turn.

A few minutes before she was due to pick up my son, my husband came home in the car. Since it was too late for me to call and say I could drive after all, I asked my husband to hide the car in the garage and to stay inside. I also explained to my son that he shouldn't mention that his father was at home.

Unfortunately, my husband forgot and was in front of our house chatting with a friend when my lift arrived. When my son returned from practice, I asked him if she had noticed.

"Yes," he replied. "She asked me which of the two men in front of the house was my father. But don't worry, I told her I didn't know."

Always be loyal to family members when they are not present. In other words, talk about others as if they were present.

Stephen R. Covey, *The Seven Habits of Highly Effective Families*

No family can hang out the sign "Nothing the matter here".

Chinese proverb

On the way to school, the doctor had left her stethoscope on the car seat, and her little girl picked it up and began playing with it.

"Be still, my heart," thought the doctor, "my daughter wants to follow in my footsteps!" Then the child spoke into the stethoscope, "Welcome to the burger drive-thru. May I take your order?"

"I'm ashamed of you," the mother said. "Fighting with your friend is a terrible thing to do!"

"He threw a stone at me!" the boy said. "So I threw one at him."

The mother stated emphatically, "When he threw a stone at you, you should have come to me."

The boy quickly replied, "What good would that have done? My aim is much better than yours!"

FASHION

Fashion has become a joke. The designers have forgotten that there are women inside the dresses. Most women dress for men and want to be admired. But they must also be able to move, to get into a car without bursting their seams! Clothes must have a natural shape.

Coco Chanel

FATHERS

A father is always making
his baby into a little woman.
And when she is a woman he
turns her back again.

Enid Bagnold

It doesn't matter who my father was; it matters who I remember he was.

Anne Sexton

The most important thing a father can do for his children is to love their mother.

Henry Ward Beecher

If mothers would understand that much of their importance lies in building up the father image for the child, the children would turn out well.

Samuel S. Liebowitz

A truly rich man is one whose children run into his arms when his hands are empty.

Anon.

A man's children and his garden both reflect the amount of weeding done during the growing season.

Anon.

What makes a dad

God took the strength of a mountain,
The majesty of a tree,
The warmth of a summer sun,
The calm of a quiet sea,
The generous soul of nature,
The comforting arm of night,
The wisdom of the ages,
The power of the eagle's flight,
The joy of a morning in spring,
The faith of a mustard seed,
The patience of eternity,
The depth of a family need,
Then God combined these qualities,
When there was nothing more to add,
He knew his masterpiece was complete,
And so,
He called it... Dad

Author unknown

Did you know that...?

An American survey revealed that only 4.1% of American teenage girls felt they could go to their father to talk about a serious problem. The most popular source of help in a crisis was music, followed by peers, and, thirdly, TV. Dads were 48th on the list, but mums didn't fare much better, coming in at 31st.

Honour your father...

Listen to your father, who gave you life...
for...a foolish child brings grief to a father...
and...there is no joy for the father of a rebel.

***The Bible*, Proverbs 23:22, 17:25 & 21**

FEAR

We put off what we fear. This is the essence of procrastination. The only antidote is to ... do it now. Do the thing you fear most ... don't waste time thinking about it, just do it.

Fiona Harrold, *Be Your Own Life Coach*

Love is what we were born with. Fear is what we learn here. The spiritual journey is the relinquishment, or unlearning, of fear and the acceptance of love back into our hearts.

Marianne Williamson

You gain strength, courage and confidence by every experience in which you really stop to look fear in the face.

Eleanor Roosevelt

I have not ceased being fearful, but I have ceased to let fear control me. I have accepted fear as a part of life – specifically the fear of change, the fear of the unknown; and I have gone ahead despite the pounding in my heart that says: turn back, turn back, you'll die if you venture too far.

Erica Jong

God is our refuge and strength, always ready to help in times of trouble. So we will not fear, even if earthquakes come and mountains fall into the sea.
***The Bible*, Psalm 46:1–2**

Nothing in life is to be feared. It is only to be understood.
Marie Curie

FEMINISM

I myself have never been able to find out precisely what feminism is: I only know that people call me a feminist whenever I express sentiments that differentiate me from a doormat.

Rebecca West (1913)

Pseudo-feminists talk aggressiveness but practise timidity. Take sexual harassment. Every time I turn on the news some woman is describing, with murky insouciance, that terrible day ten years ago when her self-esteem was shattered because her male boss kept looking at her body parts instead of her face. A real feminist would say, "I'm up here, Mr Crabtree," and that would be the end of it. If you say it right, you only have to say it once.
Florence King

Feminists react against patriarchy, but have rubbed out their own distinctive nature in the process. Post-feminism states that what a woman is has not yet emerged or really been understood.

Kevin O'Donnell, *Postmodernism*, Lion (2003)

It's important to remember that feminism is no longer a group of organisations or leaders. It's the expectations that parents have for their daughters, and their sons, too. It's the way we talk about and treat one another. It's who makes the money and who makes the compromises and who makes the dinner. It's a state of mind. It's the way we live now.

Anna Quindlen

FOOD

If you are what you eat,
then I'm fast, cheap and easy.

Anon.

Never eat more than you can lift.

Miss Piggy

Veni, Vidi, Vegi...
I came, I saw, I had a salad.

Anon.

Offerings of food have been breaking down barriers for centuries.

Estée Lauder

Allow for the weaknesses of different eaters; so that if someone cannot eat of the one dish he may still make a meal from the other.

The Rule of St Benedict

In general my children refuse to eat anything that hasn't danced on television.

Erma Bombeck

Never trust a thin chef.

Anon.

A bowl of soup with someone you love
Is better than steak with someone you hate.
A dry crust eaten in peace
is better than a great feast with strife.

***The Bible*, Proverbs 15:17 and 17:1**

FORGIVENESS

Forgiveness is an act of the will, and the will can function regardless of the temperature of the heart.

Corrie ten Boom

Forgiveness is the economy of the heart… forgiveness saves the expense of anger, the cost of hatred, the waste of spirits.

Hannah More, *Practical Piety*

Get rid of all bitterness, rage and anger… be kind to each other, tender-hearted, forgiving one another, just as God through Christ has forgiven you.

***The Bible*, Ephesians 4:31–32**

One of the secrets of a long and fruitful life is to forgive everybody everything every night before you go to bed.

Ann Landers

If you haven't forgiven yourself something, how can you forgive others?

Dolores Huerta

As long as you don't forgive, who and whatever it is will occupy rent-free space in your mind.
Isabelle Holland, *The Long Search*

FREEDOM

For you have been called to live in freedom … not freedom to satisfy your sinful nature, but freedom to serve one another in love.
St Paul, *The Bible*, Galatians 5:13

I had crossed the line, I was free; but there was no one there to welcome me to the land of freedom. I was a stranger in a strange land.
Harrlet Tubman (liberated slave)

Freedom comes in individual packages.
Shirley Boone, *One Woman's Liberation*

I am old enough to know that victory is often a thing deferred, and rarely at the summit of courage … What is at the summit of courage, I think, is freedom… the freedom that comes with the knowledge that no earthly thing can break you.
Paula Giddings

In any free society, the conflict between social conformity and individual liberty is permanent.

Kathleen Norris

If one lets fear or hate or anger take possession of the mind, they become self-forged chains.

Helen Gahagan Douglas

We must determine whether we really want freedom – whether we are willing to dare the perils of… rebirth… For we never take a step forward without surrendering something that we may have held dear, without dying to that which has been.

Virginia Hanson

If all men are born free, how is it all women are born slaves?

Mary Astell (1706)

You can't free a fish from water.

I. S. Behr,
Ferengi Rules of Acquisition

FRIENDSHIP

Treat your friends as you do your best pictures, and place them in their best light.

Jennie Jerome Churchill

A friend is someone who can see through you and still enjoys the show.

Anon.

How to make friends and keep them

Always be ready to make a friend, whatever the situation, however unlikely the person.

Be interested in other people. Have a "there you are" attitude rather than one that says "here I am".

Don't be possessive of your friends – introduce them to others.

Keep in touch with your friends; like plants, friends need nurture.

Don't expect more from your friends than you know they can offer.

Appreciate your friends for who they are, not for what they can give you.

Source unknown

Never abandon a friend... either yours or your father's.

The Bible, Proverbs 27:10

Friendship doubles our joy and divides our grief.

Swedish proverb

If we would build on a sure foundation in friendship, we must love friends for their sake rather than for our own.

Charlotte Brontë

It is very important for us to associate with others who are walking in the right way – not only those who are where we are in the journey, but also those who have gone further.

Teresa of Avila, *The Interior Castle*

You cannot shake hands with a clenched fist.

Indira Gandhi

The best way to keep a friend is not to give them away.

Anon.

I have lost friends, some by death... others through sheer inability to walk across the street.

Virginia Woolf

FULFILMENT

To love what you do and feel that it matters – how could anything be more fun?

Katherine Graham

If you please man and never please God, you have nothing. If you please God, and man forsakes you, you have everything.

Dorothy Patterson

FUTURE

Someday...

Someday, when the kids are grown up,
life will be different.
The note on my fridge door
will read, "Afternoon at hairdresser," or,
"Browse through art gallery," or, "Start golf lessons,"
instead of,
"Paediatrician at 2 pm" or, "Cub pack meeting".

Someday, when the kids are grown up,
the house will be free of graffiti.
There will be no crayoned smiley faces on the walls,
no names scrawled in furniture dust,
no pictures fingered on steamy windows,
and no initials etched in bars of soap.

Someday, when the kids are grown up,
I'll get through a whole chapter of an engrossing book
without being interrupted to sew a nose on a teddy bear,
stop a toddler from eating the dog food,
or rescue the cat from the toy box.

Someday, when the kids are grown up,
I won't find brown apple cores under the beds,
empty rolls on the toilet paper hanger,
or fuzzy caterpillars in denim jeans.
And I will be able to find a pencil in the desk drawer,
a slice of leftover cake in the fridge,
and the comics still in the centre of the newspaper.

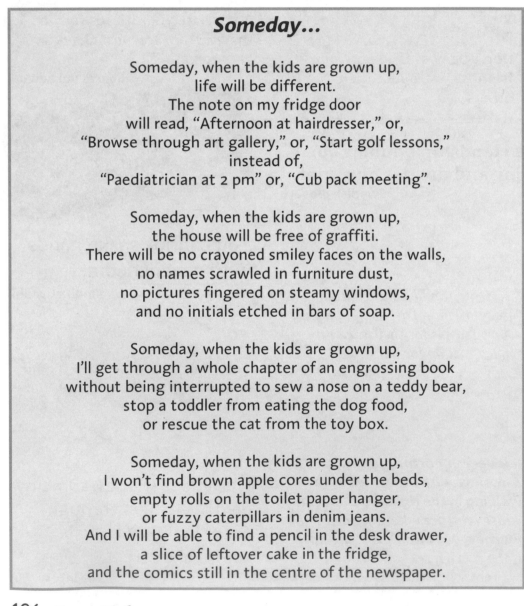

Someday, when the kids are grown up,
I'll breeze right past the sweet display in the supermarket
without having to fumble for pennies;
I'll stroll freely down each aisle without fear
of inadvertently passing the music or toy sections;
and I'll choose cereal without considering what noise it makes,
what prize it contains, or what colour it comes in.

Someday, when the kids are grown up,
I'll prepare Quiche Lorraine, or Scallops Amandine,
or just plain liver and onions, and no one will say,
"Yuk! I wish we were having hot dogs!" or,
"Jimmy's lucky, his mum lets him eat chocolate bars for dinner."
And we'll eat by candlelight,
with no one trying to roast their peas and carrots over the flame
to "make them taste better", or
arguing about who gets to blow out the candle when we've finished.

Someday, when the kids are grown up,
I'll get ready for my bath without first having to remove scuba -
diving action figures, sharks and plastic mermaids.

I'll luxuriate in hot, steamy water and billows of bubbles
for a whole hour,
and no fists will pound on the door;
no small voices will yell, "Hurry up, Mummy! I've got to go!"

Yes, someday, when the kids are grown up, life will be different.
They'll leave our nest, and the house will be
Quiet...
and calm...
and empty...
and lonely...
And I won't like that at all!
And then I'll spend my time, not looking forward to
someday, but looking back at yesterday.

As we become purer channels for God's light, we develop an appetite for the sweetness that is possible in this world. A miracle worker is not geared toward fighting what the world is, but toward creating the world that could be.

Marianne Williamson

Never be afraid to trust an unknown future to a known God.

Corrie ten Boom

Every mother is like Moses. She does not enter the Promised Land. She prepares for a world she will not see.

Pope Paul VI

Don't brag about tomorrow, since you don't know what the day will bring.

***The Bible*, Proverbs 27:1**

G

GARDENING

If all flowers wanted to be roses, nature would lose her springtime beauty, and fields would no longer be decked out with little wildflowers.

St Thérèse of Lisieux

The ultimate kitchen garden:

For the garden of your daily living

Plant three rows of peas:
1. Peace of mind
2. Peace of heart
3. Peace of soul

Plant four rows of squash:
1. Squash gossip
2. Squash indifference
3. Squash grumbling
4. Squash selfishness

Plant four rows of lettuce:
1. Lettuce be faithful
2. Lettuce be kind
3. Lettuce be patient
4. Lettuce really love one another

Plant three rows of turnips:
1. Turnip for meetings
2. Turnip for service
3. Turnip to help one another

Plant three types of thyme:
1. Thyme for each other
2. Thyme for family
3. Thyme for friends

Water freely with patience and cultivate with love, and there will be much fruit in your garden because you reap what you sow.

GENIUS

Genius lies not in thinking of ideas, but in the ability to execute the ideas.
Jane McElyea

Genius is an infinite capacity for taking life by the scruff of the neck.
Katharine Hepburn

GIFT

What we are is God's gift to us. What we become is our gift to God.
Louis Nizer

The greatest gift we can give one another is rapt attention to one another's existence.
Sue Atchley Ebaugh

The gift of God is eternal life through Christ Jesus our Lord.
***The Bible*, Romans 6:23b**

GIVING

The fragrance always stays in the hand that gives the rose.

Hada Bejar

You can give without loving, but you cannot love without giving.

Amy Carmichael

The hand that gives is never empty.

Norwegian proverb

Some people give time, some money, some their skills and connections, some literally give their life's blood. But everyone has something to give... Giving frees us from the familiar territory of our own needs by opening our mind to the unexplained worlds occupied by the needs of others.

Barbara Bush

A rejected opportunity to give is a lost opportunity to receive.

Anon.

Instead of getting hard ourselves and trying to compete, women should try to give their best qualities to men – bring them softness, teach them how to cry.

Joan Baez

Real giving is when we give to our spouses what is important to them, whether we understand it, like it, agree with it, or not.

Michele Weiner-Davis,
Divorce Busting

GLAMOUR

People are glamorous from a distance. The difficult thing is for them to remain glamorous if you know them.

Alexandra Shulman, Editor of *Vogue* speaking in *Good Housekeeping*, Jan 2003

Grown-up dressing... pared-down chic... relies far more on confidence than on the confidence trick of top-to-toe labels.

Hilary Alexander, *Telegraph Weekend*, 10 May 2003

GLORY

Look at everything as though you were seeing it either for the first or last time. Then your time on earth will be filled with glory.
Betty Smith

The greatest glory of a woman is to be least talked about by men.
Pericles (495–429 BC)

GOALS

Goal-setting tends to be a problem for women. It's easy to understand why, when you consider that... women have been taught not to be selfish, but goal-setting requires one to be focused on the self.
Marjorie Shaevitz, *The Superwoman Syndrome*

Even if I don't reach all my goals, I've gone higher than I would have if I hadn't set any.
Danielle Fotopoulis

The most notable fact that culture imprints on women is the sense of our limits. The most important thing one woman can do for another is to illuminate and expand her sense of actual possibilities.
Adrienne Rich

A woman has to look at her life objectively in terms of the kinds of obstacles she confronts, has confronted, perhaps will confront. You've got to know what you're up against.
Kathleen Noble, *Gifted Women: Identity and Expression*

GOSSIP

Never slander a person to [their] employer. If you do, the person will curse you, and you will pay for it.

***The Bible*, Proverbs 30:10**

GRACE

You have not lived a perfect day, even though you have earned money, unless you have done something for someone who will never be able to repay you.

Ruth Smeltzer

GRIEF

Hopeless grief is passionless.

Elizabeth Barrett Browning

I have permission to be human… to feel hot anger, to cry wet tears and to search again for a song in the long night… and I will be better, maybe even a better person for all this.

Kathleen Gibson, Someone I Loved Has Died, *Readers' Digest*, May 2002

Heavy hearts, like heavy clouds, are best relieved by the shedding of a little water.

Anon.

I like living. I have sometimes been wildly, despairingly, acutely miserable, racked with sorrow, but through it all I still know quite certainly that just to be alive is a grand thing.

Agatha Christie

GROWTH

Change is inevitable,
Growth is intentional.
Carolyn Coats

Life is change.
Growth is optional.
Choose wisely.
Karen Clark Kaiser

We are not born all at once, but by bits. The body first, and the spirit later; and the birth and growth of the spirit, in those who are attentive to their own inner life, are slow and exceedingly painful. Our mothers are racked with the pains of our physical birth; we ourselves suffer the longer pains of our spiritual growth.

Mary Antin (1912)

If growing up is the process of creating ideas and dreams about what life should be, then maturity is letting go again.
Mary Beth Danielson

We older women who know we aren't heroines can offer our younger sisters, at the very least, an honest report of what we have learned and how we have grown.
Elizabeth Janeway

H

HABITS

It's not what you do once in a while, it's what you do day in and day out that makes the difference.

Jenny Craig

Habit is necessary; it is the habit of having habits, of turning a trail into a rut, which must be incessantly fought against if one is to remain alive.

Edith Wharton, *A Backward Glance*

HAIR

Did you know that...?

Modern shampoos that are designed to remove styling products from your hair, will also remove them from glass!

Grey hair is a crown of glory, it is gained by a godly life.

***The Bible*, Proverbs 16:31**

HAPPINESS

Happiness is not having what you want, but wanting what you have.

Source unknown

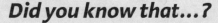

Only two things are necessary to keep one's wife happy. One is to let her think she is having her own way, and the other is to let her have it.

Lyndon B. Johnson

Everyone has the power to make someone happy –
Some by simply entering a room,
Some by quietly leaving it.

Source unknown

Happiness is not a state to arrive at, but a manner of travelling.

Margaret Lee Runbeck

Many people have a wrong idea of what constitutes true happiness. It is not attained through self-gratification, but through fidelity to a worthy purpose.

Helen Keller

God can't give happiness and peace apart from himself, because it is not there. There is no such thing.

C.S. Lewis

We all live with the objective of being happy; our lives are all different and yet the same.

Anne Frank

HATE

We must remember that hatred is like acid. It does more damage to the vessel in which it is stored than to the object on which it is poured.

Ann Landers

HEROISM

Each woman is far from average in the daily heroics of her life, even though she may never receive a moment's recognition in history.

***Women and Work*, Newsage Press**

A hero is one who knows how to hang on one minute longer.

Norwegian proverb

HESITATION

To think too long about doing a thing often becomes its undoing.

Eva Young

HOLINESS

Our holiness is an effect, not a cause; as long as our eyes are on our own personal whiteness as an end in itself, the thing breaks down. God can do nothing while my interest is in my personal character – he will take care of this if I obey his call.

Florence Allshorn

HOME

A sense of home is about people rather than place, so my home is created by and for my family.

Sheila Teague, *Good Housekeeping*, June 2003

A few children or a pet create a sense of home and guarantee you don't become too serious.

Paul Costelloe, *Good Housekeeping*, June 2003

HONESTY

It is an honour to receive an honest reply.

The Bible, Proverbs 24:26

There's nothing more dangerous than an honest businessman.

I. S. Behr, *The Ferengi Rules of Acquisition*

HOPE

Expect to have hope rekindled.
Expect your prayers to be answered in wondrous ways.
The dry seasons in life do not last.
The spring rains will come again.

Sarah Ban Breathnach

Just as despair can come to one only from other human beings, hope, too, can be given to one only by other human beings.

Elie Wiesel

HOSPITALITY

A vicar and his wife decided to have the churchwardens and their wives to dinner. When it was time for the meal, everyone was seated and the vicar's wife asked her little four-year-old daughter if she would say grace.

The girl said, "I don't know what to say."

Her mum then told her, "Just say what I say."

So everyone bowed their head and the little girl said, "O dear Lord, why am I having all these people over for dinner? Amen!"

HOUSEWORK

The major reason women don't get help with housework is they don't ask for it.

Diana Silcox with Mary Ellen Moore, *Woman Time*

I hate housework. You make the beds, you wash the dishes and six months later you have to start all over again.

Joan Rivers

Conran's Law of Housework – it expands to fill the time available plus half an hour.

Shirley Conran, *Superwoman 2*

Bride: **How can I keep my wedding ring clean?**
Mother: **Soak it gently in dishwater three times a day.**

I'm not going to vacuum 'til they make one you can ride on.

Roseanne Barr

Did you know that… ?

Research recently undertaken by a British insurance company has shown that mothers spend on average 64 hours a week cooking, ironing, sewing and other domestic tasks. If that was not enough, two-thirds of the women interviewed also went out to work, although not all of them full-time. It was estimated it would cost a household over £20,000 per year to pay someone to perform a mother's domestic tasks on her behalf. Amazingly, only 8% of the women interviewed had an insurance policy that would cover these costs in the event of their death.

Housework – a real definition

Housework is the sum of unpaid labour performed by household members which serves one or more of the following purposes:

1. Providing household members' physical and/or psychological sustenance.
2. Enabling household members to meet institutional commitments outside the household, such as doing paid work or going to school.
3. Producing a good or service used by household members.
4. Maintaining a quality of household life "reasonably" expected within the culture, class and/or community in which the household is situated.
5. Acquiring foods or services necessary to accomplish any of the above purposes from sources outside the household.
6. Organising or facilitating any of the above purposes.

Joanne C. May Kliejunas, *Being of Use: The Value of Housework in the Household and the Economy.* PhD thesis, Stanford Univ., 1982

The last fight we had was my fault. My wife asked, "What's on the TV?" I said, "Dust!"

What happened here today, darling?

One evening a man came home from work to find total mayhem in the house. His three children were in the garden still in their pyjamas, playing in the mud, with empty food boxes and wrappers strewn all around.

Walking into the lounge, he found an even bigger mess. A lamp had been knocked over, the TV was blaring out a cartoon channel, and toys and various items of clothing were scattered all over the floor.

In the kitchen, dishes filled the sink, breakfast food was spilled on the counter, dog food was spilled on the floor, a broken glass lay under the table and a small pile of sand was spread by the back door.

He quickly headed up the stairs, stepping over toys and piles of clothes, looking for his wife. He was worried she might be ill, or that something serious had happened.

He found her lounging in the bedroom, still curled up in the bed in her pyjamas, reading a novel. She looked up at him, smiled, and asked how his day went. He looked at her, bewildered, and asked, "What happened here today?"

She again smiled and answered, "You know every day when you come home from work and ask me what in the world did I do today?"

"Yes," was his incredulous reply.

"Well, this is it," she replied.

HUMILITY

Humility is attentive patience.

Simone Weil, *First and Last Notebooks*

[S]he who is humble is confident and wise.
[S]he who brags is insecure and lacking.

Lisa Edmondson

To live and let live, without clamour for distinction or recognition; to wait on divine love; to write truth first on the table of one's own heart – this is the sanity and perfection of living, and my human ideal.

Mary Baker Eddy

HUSBANDS

Q: How do you keep your husband from reading your e-mail?

A: Rename the mail folder to "instruction manuals".

Advice for wives:

Be to his virtues very kind.
Be to his faults a little blind.

Anon.

I'd go to the end of the world for my husband. Of course, if he'd just stop and ask directions, I wouldn't have to.

Martha Bolton, *I Love You Still*

An archaeologist is the best husband a woman can have: the older she gets, the more interested he is in her.

Agatha Christie

The only thing worse than a husband who never notices what you cook or what you wear, is a husband who always notices what you wear or what you cook.

Sandra Litoff

I

IDENTITY

We don't know
who we are
until we see
what we can do.
Martha Grimes

Defining myself, as opposed to being defined by others, is one of the most difficult challenges I face.
Carol Mosely-Braun

IMAGINATION

The key to life is imagination. If you don't have that, no matter what you have, it's meaningless. If you do have imagination ... you can make feast of straw.
Jane Stanton Hitchcock

Imagination is the highest
kite one can fly.
Lauren Bacall

IMPOSSIBILITIES

NOTHING IS IMPOSSIBLE WITH GOD
The Bible, Luke 1:37

When work, commitment and pleasure all become one and you reach that deep well where passion lives, nothing is impossible.
Nancy Coey

The word "impossible" is not in heaven's dictionary.
Mark Stibbe

You do not test the resources of God until you attempt the impossible.
F. B. Meyer

Something which we think is impossible now is not impossible in another decade.
Constance Baker Motley, First black woman in the USA to become a Federal Judge

Aerodynamically the bumblebee shouldn't be able to fly, but the bumblebee doesn't know that, so it goes on flying anyway.
Mary Kay Ash

INDIFFERENCE

Indifference is the strongest force in the universe. It makes everything it touches meaningless. Love and hate don't stand a chance against it.
Joan Vinge, *The Snow Queen*

Science may have found a cure for most evils; but it has found no remedy for the worst of them all – the apathy of human beings.
Helen Keller

When good people in any country cease their vigilance and struggle, then evil men prevail.
Pearl S. Buck

The sad truth is that most evil is done by people who never make up their minds to be good or evil.
Hannah Arendt

The opposite of love is not hate, it's indifference.
The opposite of art is not ugliness, it's indifference.
The opposite of faith is not heresy, it's indifference.
And the opposite of life is not death, it's indifference.
Elie Wiesel

INFERIORITY

Nobody can make you feel inferior without your permission.

Eleanor Roosevelt

The woman who feels that she is nothing unless she is constantly giving, who is in constant need of reassurance, or who falls into the martyr role…creates misery for others as well as herself.

Grace Baruch, Rosalind Barnett and Caryl Rivers, *Lifeprints* (New York: McGraw-Hill, 1983, p.30)

INNER PEACE

The problem is not entirely in finding the room of one's own, the time alone, difficult and necessary as that is. The problem is more how to still the soul in the midst of its activities.

Anne Morrow Lindbergh,
Gift from the Sea

Nothing is more important than taking time to know yourself once again, giving yourself the space for self-revelation to take place.

Tama J. Kieves,
This Time I Dance

How to get inner peace …

A friend sent me an article that said the way to achieve inner peace is to finish things you've started. It's definitely working for me. I am now making a point of always finishing whatever I've started and I think I am well on the way toward finding inner peace.

Because I care for you, I am passing this wisdom on to you. Here are the things I finished today:

- Two bags of crisps
- A strawberry cheesecake
- A packet of chocolate biscuits
- A bottle of non-diet fizzy drink
- A small box of chocolates I found under the sofa from Christmas.

I think I feel better already!

INSANITY

Insanity is hereditary – you catch it from your children.

Anon.

INSOMNIA

Insomnia is a disease transmitted to adults by babies and small children.

Anon.

INSPIRATION

A man was asked to describe his life with his wife.

"She has displayed an extraordinary amount of patience," he answered. He paused, and then continued, "Women are an inspiration. It's because of them we put on clean shirts and wash our necks. Because of women, men want to excel; because of a woman, Columbus discovered America."

"Queen Isabella," murmured his wife.

"I was thinking of Mrs Columbus," he said, deadpan.

INTELLIGENCE

My professor at Bristol University told me I would have to work extra hard to be taken seriously because I was attractive.

Dr Charlotte Uhlenbroek, *Radio Times*

Whatever women do, they must do twice as well as men to be thought half as good.

Charlotte Whitton

I'm not offended by all the dumb blonde jokes because I know I'm not dumb... and I also know that I'm not blonde.

Dolly Parton

As soon as a woman thinks sufficiently fast, one calls it intuition.

Barbro Alving

INVOLVEMENT

When you do nothing, you feel overwhelmed and powerless. But when you get involved, you feel the sense of hope and accomplishment that comes from knowing you are working to make things better.

Pauline R. Kezer

When you cease to make a contribution you begin to die.

Eleanor Roosevelt

IRRITATION

There once was an oyster whose story I'll tell,
Who found a grain of sand had got under her shell;
Just one little grain, but it gave her much pain,
For oysters have feelings although they're so plain.
Now, did she berate the working of Fate
That had led her to such a deplorable state?
No – as she lay on the shelf, she said to herself,
"If I cannot remove it, I'll try to improve it."

So the years rolled by as the years always do,
And she came to her ultimate destiny – stew.
And this small grain of sand which had bothered her so,
Was a beautiful pearl, all richly aglow.
Now this tale has a moral – for isn't it grand
What an oyster can do with a morsel of sand;
What couldn't we do if we'd only begin
With all of the things that get under our skin.

Author unknown

KINDNESS

When you are kind to someone in trouble, you hope they'll remember and be kind to someone else. And it'll become like a wildfire.
Whoopi Goldberg

The great acts of love are done by those who are habitually performing small acts of kindness.
Anon.

But you must be reasonable and kind to yourself. Women are not often good at being kind to themselves.
Elizabeth Buchan, *The Good Wife*

KNOWLEDGE

Don't let anyone lead you astray with empty philosophy and high-sounding nonsense that come from human thinking...

St Paul, *The Bible*, Colossians 2:8

If you have knowledge, let others light their candles in it.

Margaret Fuller

L

LAUGHTER

The most wasted of all days is that on which one has not laughed.

Ralph Waldo Emerson

If you're going to be able to look back on something and laugh about it, you might as well laugh about it now.

Marie Osmond

Moonlight and roses are bound to fade
for every lover and every maid;
but the bond that holds in any weather
is learning how to laugh together.

Source unknown

Laugh a little now and then
It brightens life a lot;
You can see the brighter side
Just as well as not.
Don't go mournfully around,
Gloomy and forlorn;
Try to make your fellow (wo)men
Glad that you were born.

Author unknown

Did you know that...?

It takes more muscles to frown than it does to smile.

Laugh at yourself...
before anyone else can.

Elsa Maxwell

She who laughs, lasts.

Mary Pettibone Poole

Did you know that...?

The average child laughs about 400 times per day, the average adult laughs only 15 times per day. What happened to the other 385 laughs?

USA Today

LEADERSHIP

I'm honoured to be the first woman to have the opportunity to command the shuttle. I don't really think about that on a day-to-day basis because I really don't need to.

Air Force Col. Eileen Collins, first female space shuttle commander, 24 June 1999

A leader
takes people where they want to go.
A great leader
takes people where they don't necessarily want to go,
but ought to be.

Rosalynn Carter

LIABILITY

After a woman sued a fast-food chain because she wasn't warned her coffee was boiling hot, it seems that companies are changing their instruction manuals and product warning labels to cover themselves from product liability.

Here are some of the more ludicrous ones:

- On a bar of soap – Directions: Use like regular soap.
- Frozen dinner – Suggestion: Defrost before eating.
- Bread pudding from well-known supermarket – Product will be hot after heating.
- Electric iron – Caution, do not iron clothes on body.
- On a string of Christmas lights – For indoor or outdoor use only.
- Supermarket-brand peanuts warn – May contain peanuts.
- On a blanket made in the far east – Not to be used as protection from a tornado.
- On a motorcycle-helmet-mounted mirror – Remember, objects in the mirror are actually behind you.
- On an insect spray – This product is not tested on animals.
- On a luxury frozen dessert with defrosting instructions on the underside of the box – Keep upright.
- On the bottle top of a flavoured milk drink – After opening, keep upright.

LIBERATION

Nothing liberates our greatness like the desire to help, the desire to serve.

Marianne Williamson

One of the reasons I don't see eye to eye with Women's Lib. is that women have it all on a plate if only they knew it. They don't have to be pretty either.

Charlotte Rampling

I reasoned this out in my mind, there were two things I had a right to – liberty and death. If I could not have one I would have the other; for no one should take me alive.

Harriet Tubman 1820–1913
(Born a slave, but led 300 slaves to freedom)

LIES

If you tell a lie, don't believe it deceives only the other person.

Anon.

We must be careful not to lie to ourselves. It is very easy to deceive ourselves about the reality and consequences of our actions.

Mary Pytches, *Between Friends*

Lying is done with words and also with silence.

Adrienne Rich

The secret in life is that everyone must sew it for themselves.

Søren Kierkegaard,
Fear and Trembling

Crowding a life does not always enrich it.

Anon.

I wanted a perfect ending. Now I've learned, the hard way, that some poems don't rhyme, and some stories don't have a clear beginning, middle and end. Life is about not knowing, having to change, taking the moment and making the best of it, without knowing what's going to happen next.

Gilda Radner

Life should be measured by its breadth, not its length.

Anon.

Life is either a tightrope or a feather bed – give me the tightrope.

Edith Wharton

It may be that life can only be understood backwards, but it has to be lived forwards.

Søren Kierkegaard, ***The Sickness unto Death***

Real life isn't always going to be perfect or go our way, but the recurring acknowledgement of what is working in our lives can help us not only to survive but surmount our difficulties.

Sarah Ban Breathnach

LISTENING

The most basic and powerful way to connect to another person is to listen. Just listen. Perhaps the most important thing we ever give each other is our attention… A loving silence often has far more power to heal and to connect than the most well-intentioned words.

Rachel Naomi Remen

How do the geese know when to fly to the sun? Who tells them the seasons? How do we, humans, know when it is time to move on? As with the migrant birds, so surely with us, there is a voice within, if only we would listen to it, that tells us so certainly when to go forth into the unknown.

Elisabeth Kübler-Ross

LONELINESS

When they are alone they want to be with others, and when they are with others they want to be alone. After all, human beings are like that.

Gertrude Stein

No one would choose a friendless existence on condition of having all the other things in the world.

Aristotle

The loneliest woman in the world is a woman without a close woman friend.

George Santayana, *The Life of Reason*, 1905–06

Loneliness is the poverty of self; solitude is the richness of self.

May Sarton

The person who tries to live alone will not succeed as a human being. His heart withers if it does not answer another heart. His mind shrinks away if he hears only the echoes of his own thoughts and finds no other inspiration.

Pearl S. Buck

There is absolutely no point sitting around feeling sorry for yourself. The great power you have is to let go ... focus on what you have, not that which has been mean, or unkindly removed.

Minnie Driver

When Christ said, "I was hungry and you fed me," he didn't mean only hunger for bread and for food; he also meant the hunger to be loved. Jesus himself experienced this loneliness. He came amongst his own and his own received him not, and it hurt him then and it has kept on hurting him. The same hunger, the same loneliness, the same having no one to be accepted by, and to be loved and wanted by. Every human being in that case resembles Christ in his loneliness; and that is the hardest part, that's real hunger.

Mother Teresa

If someone listens, or stretches out a hand, or whispers a word of encouragement, or attempts to understand a lonely person, extraordinary things begin to happen.

Loretta Girzartis

LOVE

Love is the time and space where "I" give myself the right to be extraordinary.

Julia Kristeva, *Tales of Love*

The love of our neighbour in all its fullness simply means being able to say, "What are you going through?"

Simone Weil

How do you show your man you really love him?

An informal survey asked participants what they wished their woman would do to express her love. Here are the results:

- Appreciate the things I do rather than focusing on the things I don't do.
- Be my greatest supporter.
- Take more initiative to set up special times together.
- Accept my weaknesses and love me unconditionally.
- Allow me some time to myself.
- Express appreciation when I help you.
- Be spontaneous with hugs, kisses and saying, "I love you".
- Give me a chance to drop my briefcase, say "hi" and relax before you give me your concerns and problems.
- Cook my favourite meal.
- Greet me with a smile.
- Make a big deal about my birthday.
- Gently correct me in private rather than contradicting me in front of others.
- Just listen to me without assuming what I'm thinking or about to say. Don't interrupt.

Love is a four-letter word spelled **T-I-M-E**

The ultimate lesson all of us have to learn is unconditional love, which includes not only others but ourselves as well.
Elisabeth Kübler-Ross

Love is patient and kind.
Love is not jealous or boastful or proud or rude.
Love does not demand its own way.
Love is not irritable, and it keeps no record of when it has been wronged.
It is never glad about injustice but rejoices whenever the truth wins out.
Love never gives up, never loses faith, is always hopeful, and endures through every circumstance.

St Paul, *The Bible*, 1 Corinthians 13:4–7

A day without a kiss is a day wasted.

Allison Pearson, "Sacrifice is written in our genes", *Good Housekeeping*, June 2003

We are so preciously loved by God that we cannot even comprehend it. No created being can ever know how much and how sweetly and tenderly God loves them…it is our nature to long for him, and it is his nature to long for us.

Julian of Norwich, *Revelations of Divine Love*

Love has nothing to do with what you are expecting to get – only with what you are expecting to give – which is everything.

Katharine Hepburn

Love doesn't commit suicide. We have to kill it. It often simply dies of our neglect.

Diane Sollee, smartmarriages.com

Love is the great purifier of life.

Andy Economides

PRINCESS,
HAVING HAD SUFFICIENT SUCCESS WITH PRINCES,
SEEKS FROG.

A child's view of love

"When my gran got arthritis, she couldn't bend over and paint her toenails any more. So my grandpa does it for her all the time, even when his hands got arthritis too. That's love." Rebecca, age 8.

"Love is when you go out to eat and give somebody most of your chips without making them give you any of theirs." Chrissy, age 6.

"Love is what makes you smile when you're tired." Terri, age 4.

"Love is when my mummy makes coffee for my daddy and she takes a sip before giving it to him, to make sure the taste is OK." Danny, age 7.

"Love is when you tell a guy you like his shirt, and then he wears it every day." Noelle, age 7.

"Love is when mummy gives daddy the best piece of chicken." Elaine, age 5.

"Love is when your puppy licks your face even after you left him alone all day." Mary Ann, age 4.

Source unknown

If grass can grow through cement, Love can find you anywhere.

Cher

MARRIAGE

Marriage is a career which brings about more benefits than many others.

Simone de Beauvoir

Marriage is like a duet: we need not play the same part, but we must be playing in harmony.

Anon.

The three stages of love and marriage:

You don't know them, but you love them.
You know them, and don't love them.
You know them and you love them.

Source unknown

The difference between a successful marriage and an unsuccessful one is leaving just a few things unsaid each day.

Anon.

Marriage is an institution in which a man loses his bachelor's degree and the woman gets her master's.

J. John

A happy marriage is a long conversation that always seems too short.

André Maurois

Ten rules for a happy marriage

1. Never both be angry at the same time.
2. Never yell at each other unless the house is on fire.
3. If one of you has to win an argument, let it be your mate.
4. If you must criticise, do it lovingly.
5. Never bring up mistakes of the past.
6. Neglect the whole world rather than each other.
7. Never go to sleep with an argument unsettled.
8. At least once every day say a kind or complimentary word to your life partner.
9. When you have done something wrong, admit it and ask for forgiveness.
10. Remember it takes two to make a quarrel.

"Don't compete – complete."
Mark Stibbe

A happy marriage is like a ship in a storm at sea – the voyagers do not jump overboard at the first blow of the tempest.

R.W. Burns

Remember you are a team. You are not working independently of one another.

Janette Oke

...marriage is like a tiny rowing boat with only two oarsmen setting out on a vast uncharted ocean...

Jilly Cooper, *Daily Mail*, May 31, 2003

66 years and still holding on!

There were a couple of old guys talking at the bar. One of the men had been married for 66 years.

"Amazing. 66 years!" said his friend. "What's the secret to such a long, happy marriage?"

"Well," he replied, "It's like this. The man makes all the big decisions…and the woman just makes the little decisions."

"Really?" his friend responded. "Does that really work?"

"Oh, yes," he said proudly. "66 years, and so far, not one big decision!"

We owe it to each other, in the context of marriage, to give ourselves fully.

Phil Baker, *Letters to a Lady*

***Marriage halves our grief,
doubles our joys
and quadruples our expenses.***

Anon.

What is probably wrong today is that we expect a marriage or a relationship to be happy and successful all the time. We forget that people who have lived together for 50 years cannot have been happy every single day.

Queen Margrethe II of Denmark,
Daily Telegraph

Being married is like having someone permanently in your corner, it feels limitless, not limited.

Gloria Steinem (2000, upon marrying for the first time at the age of 66.)

What holds a marriage together is the creaking of bed springs – from laughter rather than sex.

Jilly Cooper, *Telegraph Magazine*, 24 May 2003

Getting married is the boldest and most idealistic thing that most of us will ever do.

Maggie Gallagher, *The Case for Marriage*

Never marry a man who hates his mother, because he'll end up hating you.

Jill Bennett, *The Observer*, 12 September 1982

Marriage is not just spiritual communion, it is remembering to take out the trash.

Joyce Brothers

A man and a woman, who have never met before, find themselves assigned to the same sleeping room on a transcontinental train.

Though initially embarrassed and uneasy over sharing a room, the two are tired and fall asleep quickly – he in the upper bunk and she in the lower.

At 2 am, he leans over and gently wakes the woman, saying, "I'm sorry to bother you, but would you be willing to reach into the cupboard and get me a second blanket? I'm awfully cold."

"I have a better idea," she replies. "Just for tonight, let's pretend that we're married."

"Wow! That's a great idea!!" he exclaims.

"Good," she replies. "Get your own blanket."

MEN

Men are what their mothers made them.

Ralph Waldo Emerson

The average man is more interested in a woman who is interested in him than he is in a woman – any woman – with beautiful legs.

Marlene Dietrich

Show me a woman who doesn't feel guilt and I'll show you a man.

Erica Jong

MIDDLE AGE

Ultimately the best thing about life for the middle-aged woman is living without fear. Having been through painful episodes, we know we can cope.

Elizabeth Buchan,
***Woman & Home*, May 2003**

Did you know that… ?

It is claimed that a radical diet is not required to battle middle-aged spread. American research claims that cutting out two biscuits a day, i.e. 100 calories, will halt the 2 lb 6 oz annual weight gain common to middle age. 100 calories is the equivalent of a daily walk of a mile!

At mid-life, you have to clean up any unfinished business – the back log of unprocessed emotions... there is a clarity of vision that comes at mid-life and both men and women can experience their truest selves.

Dr Christiane Northrup, "Men, the Menopause and Great Mid-life Sex", *Woman & Home*, May 2003

One of the many things nobody ever tells you about middle age is that it's such a nice change from being young.

Dorothy Canfield Fisher

I have enjoyed greatly the second blooming that comes when you finish the life of the emotions and of personal relations; and suddenly find – at the age of 50, say – that a whole new life has opened before you, filled with things you can think about, study, or read about... It is as if a fresh sap of ideas and thoughts was rising in you.

Agatha Christie

MIND

Let God transform you into a new person by changing the way you think.

St Paul, *The Bible*, Romans 12:2

Our minds work like a garden. It is fertile ground that accepts any and everything we plant. Good or evil, constructive or destructive, our lives will bear the fruit of the seeds we plant in our minds.

Ivanla Vanzant

A woman's mind is cleaner than a man's. She changes it more often.

Oliver Herford

MISTAKES

Mistakes are part of the dues one pays for a full life.

Sophia Loren

Just about the time you think you can make both ends meet, somebody moves the ends.

Pansy Penner

Pennies do not come from heaven – they have to be earned here on earth.

Margaret Thatcher

What money can't buy...

It can buy a house
But not a home

It can buy a bed
But not sleep

It can buy a clock
But not time

It can buy you a book
But not knowledge

It can buy you a position
But not respect

It can buy you medicine
But not health

It can buy you blood
But not life

It can buy you sex
But not love

So you see money isn't everything.
And it often causes pain and suffering.

Source unknown

We should so provide for old age that it may have no urgent wants of this world to absorb it from meditation on the next.

Pearl S. Buck

Did you know that...?

16% of the British population now suffer from a phobia named *financial phobia*...a crippling fear of opening bank statements and bills.

Money does not corrupt people. What corrupts people is lack of affection... Money is simply the bandage which wounded people put on their wounds.

Margaret Halsey

O God... give me neither poverty nor riches!
Give me just enough to satisfy my needs.
For if I grow rich, I may deny you and say,
"Who is the Lord?"
And if I am too poor, I may steal
and thus insult God's holy name.

A prayer from *The Bible*, Proverbs 30:8–9

MOTHERHOOD

God knows that a mother needs fortitude and courage and tolerance and flexibility and patience and firmness and nearly every other brave aspect of the human soul. But because I happen to be a parent of almost fiercely maternal nature, I praise casualness – it seems to me the rarest of virtues. It is useful enough when children are small. It is important to the point of necessity when they are adolescents.

Phyllis McGinley

You know you're a mum when…

1. You automatically double-knot everything you tie.
2. You find yourself humming the "Bob the Builder" song as you do the dishes.
3. You hear a baby cry in the supermarket, and you start to gently sway back and forth, back and forth. However, your children are at school!
4. You can never go to the toilet without someone screaming outside the door.
5. You actually start to like the smell of strained carrots mixed with apple sauce.
6. You weep through the scene in *Dumbo* when his mother is taken away, not to mention what *Bambi* does to you.
7. You actually start understanding the Klingon language.
8. You get so into crafts you contemplate writing a book called "101 Fun Crafts to do with dried pasta and PVA glue".
9. You spend half an hour searching for your sunglasses only to have your teenager say, "Mum, why don't you wear the ones you pushed up on your head?"
10. You are out for a nice romantic meal with your husband, enjoying some real adult conversation, when suddenly you realise that you've reached over and started to cut up his steak!

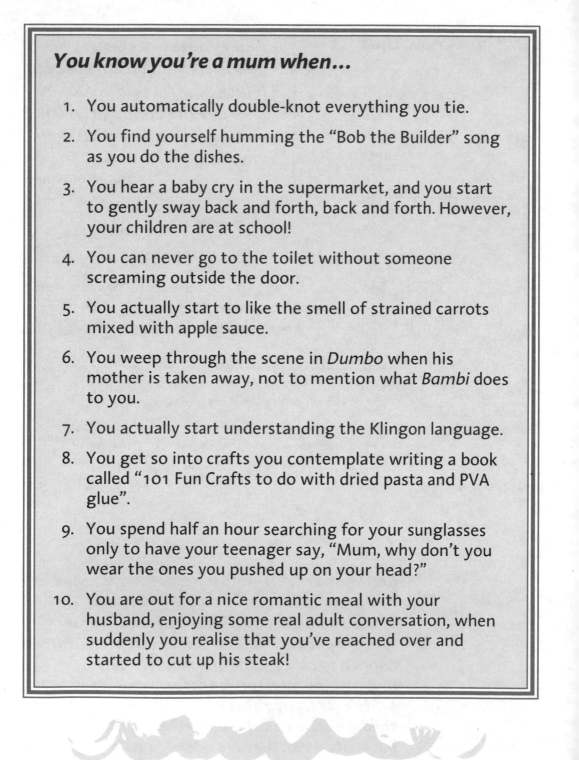

The bathroom door

The loo door is closed!

Please don't stand here and talk, whine or ask questions.

Wait until I get out.

Yes, it's locked. I want it that way. It's not broken, and I'm not trapped.

I know I've left it unlocked, and even open, since you were born – because I was afraid some horrible tragedy might occur while I was in there. But you are ten years old now, and I want some privacy.

Don't ask how long I'll be; I'll come out when I've finished.

Don't bring the phone to the door.

Don't yell down the phone that I'm on the loo.

Don't stick your fingers under the door and wiggle them – that was only funny when you were two.

Don't slide pennies and Lego or notes under the door.

If you have followed me down the hall talking, and are still talking to this closed door, please turn around and go away. I'll happily listen to you when I've finished.

And, yes, I do still love you.

Mum

The three bears...

It was a sunny morning in the big forest and the bear family was just waking up. Baby Bear went downstairs and sat in his small chair at the table. He looked into his small bowl. It was empty! "Who's been eating my porridge?" he squeaked.

Daddy Bear arrived at the table and sat in his big chair. He looked into his big bowl. It was also empty! "Who's been eating my porridge?" he roared.

Mummy Bear put her head through the serving hatch from the kitchen and yelled, "For Pete's sake, how many times do we have to go through this? It was Mummy Bear who got up first. It was Mummy Bear who woke everybody else in the house up. It was Mummy Bear who unloaded the dishwasher from last night and put everything away. It was Mummy Bear who went out into the cold early morning air to fetch the newspaper. It was Mummy Bear who set the table. It was Mummy Bear who put the cat out, cleaned the litter box and filled the cat's water and food dish. And now that you've decided to come downstairs and grace me with your presence... listen up, because I'm only going to say this one more time... I haven't made the porridge yet!

A woman is the full circle. Within her is the power to create, nurture and transform.

Diane Mariechild

I attribute my success in life to the moral, intellectual and physical education I received from my mother.

George Washington

Mothers...
...if you want breakfast in bed, sleep in the kitchen.

Allison Pearson, "Sacrifice is written in our Genes", *Good Housekeeping*, June 2003

Things my mother taught me

To appreciate a job well done: "If you're going to kill each other, do it outside – I've just finished cleaning!"

Religion: "You'd better pray that will come out of the carpet."

Time travel: "If you don't tidy up that mess, I'm going to knock you into the middle of next week!"

Logic: "Because I said so, that's why."

Further logic: "If you fall out of that swing and break your neck, you're not going to the shops with me."

Foresight: "Make sure you wear clean underwear in case you're in an accident."

Irony: "Keep crying and I'll give you something to cry about."

Osmosis: "Shut your mouth and eat your supper!"

Contortionism: "Will you 'look' at the dirt on the back of your neck!"

Stamina: "You'll sit there until all that spinach is finished."

Weather: "It looks as if a tornado has swept through your room."

Physics problems: "If I yelled because I saw a meteor coming toward you, would you listen *then*?"

Hypocrisy: "If I've told you once, I've told you a million times – don't exaggerate!"

Behavior modification: "Stop acting like your father!"

Envy: "There are millions of less fortunate children in this world who don't have wonderful parents like you do!"

Anticipation: "Just wait until we get home."

Receiving: "You are going to get it when we get home!"

Medical science: "If you don't stop crossing your eyes, they are going to freeze that way."

Think ahead: "If you don't pass your spelling test, you'll never get a good job."

Humour: "When that lawnmower cuts off your toes, don't come running to me."

Become an adult: "If you don't eat your vegetables, you'll never grow up."

Sex: "How do you think you got here?"

Genetics: "You're just like your father."

Roots: "Do you think you were born in a barn?"

Wisdom of age: "When you get to be my age, you will understand."

Justice: "One day you'll have kids... and I hope they turn out just like you!"

What their mothers might have said...

Mary, Mary, quite contrary's mother: "I don't mind you having a garden, Mary, but does it have to be growing under your bed?"

Mona Lisa's mother: "After all that money your father and I spent on braces, Mona, that's the biggest smile you can give us?"

Humpty Dumpty's mother: "Humpty, if I've told you once, I've told you a hundred times not to sit on that wall. But would you listen to me? Noooo!"

Columbus' mother: "I don't care what you've discovered, Christopher. You still could have written!"

Michelangelo's mother: "Mike, can't you paint on walls like other children? Do you have any idea how hard it is to get that stuff off the ceiling?"

Napoleon's mother: "All right, Napoleon. If you aren't hiding your school report inside your jacket, then take your hand out of there and prove it!"

Barney's mother: "I realise strained plums are your favourite, Barney, but you're starting to look a little purple."

Mary's mother: "I'm not upset that your lamb followed you to school, Mary, but I would like to know how he got better marks than you."

Batman's mother: "It's a nice car, Bruce, but do you realise how much the insurance is going to be?"

Goldilocks' mother: "I've got a bill here for a broken chair from the Bear family. You know anything about this, Goldie?"

Little Miss Muffet's mother: "Well, all I've got to say is if you don't get off your tuffet and start cleaning your room, there'll be a lot more spiders around here!"

Jonah's mother: "That's a nice story, but now tell me where you've really been for the last three days."

Superman's mother: "Clark, your father and I have discussed it, and we've decided you can have your own telephone line. Now will you stop spending so much time in all those phone booths?"

Thomas Edison's mother: "Of course I'm proud that you invented the electric light bulb, Thomas. Now turn off that light and go to bed!"

CRISPS

N

NAGGING

Nagging is the repetition of unpalatable truths.

Baroness Edith Summerskill

A nagging wife is as annoying as the constant dripping on a rainy day. Trying to stop her complaints is like trying to stop the wind or hold something with greased hands.

***The Bible*, Proverbs 27:15–16**

NEEDS

It is written, "Distribution was made to each as they had need." By this we do not say that favouritism should be shown to persons, far from it, but that infirmities should be allowed for. If someone needs less they should thank God and not be upset; if another needs more they should be humble about their weakness, and not feel important on account of the consideration shown them, and thus all members will be at peace.

The Rule of St Benedict

The different needs of men and women

The five main things women need are:

1. Affection
2. Conversation
3. Honesty and openness
4. Financial support
5. Family commitment.

The five main things men need are:

1. Sexual fulfilment
2. Recreational companionship
3. An attractive spouse
4. Domestic support
5. Admiration.

Your Father knows exactly what you need even before you ask him.

Jesus, *The Bible*, Matthew 6:8

O

OPPORTUNITY

The sad truth is that opportunity doesn't knock twice. You can put things off until tomorrow, but tomorrow may never come.

Gloria Estefan

P

PARENTS

A SLAVISH BONDAGE TO PARENTS CRAMPS EVERY FACULTY OF THE MIND.
Mary Wollstonecraft, *A Vindication of the Rights of Woman* (1792)

PATIENCE

We could never learn to be brave and patient if there were only joy in the world.
Helen Keller

Patience is bitter,
But its fruit is sweet.
Lida Clarkson, "Brush Studies", *Ladies Home Journal*, 1884

Patience can persuade a prince, and soft speech can crush strong opposition.
The Bible, Proverbs 25:15

Peace is necessary to this vast empire.
We need population, not devastation.

Catherine the Great

Fill your mind with the meaningless stimuli of a world filled with meaningless things, and it will not be easy to feel peace in your heart.

Marianne Williamson

Mankind must remember that peace is not God's gift to his creatures, peace is our gift to each other.

Elie Wiesel

Having the wisdom to face the truth will bring us closer to peace.

Melody Beattie,
Journey to the Heart

If we have no peace, it is because we have forgotten that we belong to each other.

Mother Teresa

PERCEPTION

The minute you alter your perception of yourself and your future, both you and your future begin to change.

Marilee Zdenek

If you can keep your head when all about you are losing theirs, it's just possible you haven't grasped the situation.

Jean Kerr,
Please Don't Eat the Daisies

PERFECTION

Perfection, in a Christian sense, means becoming mature enough to give ourselves to others.

Kathleen Norris

PERFECTIONISM

Perfectionism is not a malady; it is a tool of self-development.

Dr Linda Kreger Silverman, "Perfectionism: The Crucible of Giftedness", in *Advanced Development*, Volume 8, 1999

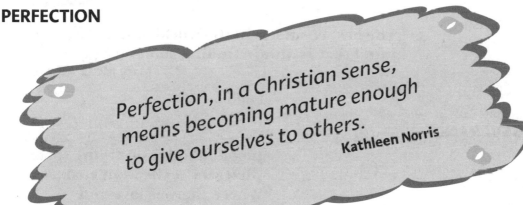

PERFUME AND MAKE-UP

There is no cosmetic for beauty like happiness.
Marguerite Gardiner Blessington

A good reputation is more valuable than the most expensive perfume.
***The Bible*, Ecclesiastes 7:1**

Make-up needn't be seen as a correction or something to hide behind. I see it as another form of expression and acceptance, even pleasure, of being in one's skin.
Kay Montano (make-up artist), *Sunday Times*, "Style"

The best cosmetic in the world is an active mind that is always finding something new.
Mary Meek Atkeson

PERSEVERANCE

Life is not easy for any of us. But what of that? We must have perseverance and above all confidence in ourselves. We must believe we are gifted for something and that this thing must be attained.
Marie Curie

Just don't give up trying to do what you really want to do. Where there is love and inspiration, I don't think you can go wrong.
Ella Fitzgerald

The great thing and the hard thing is to stick to things when you have outlived the first interest and not yet reached the second, which comes with a sort of mastery.
Janet Erskine Stuart, *Life and Letters of Janet Erskine Stuart*

How to give your cat a pill

1. Grasp cat firmly in your arms. Cradle its head on your elbow, just as if you were giving a baby a bottle. Coo confidently, "That's a nice kitty." Drop pill into its mouth.
2. Retrieve cat from top of lamp and pill from under sofa.
3. Follow same procedure as in 1, but hold cat's front paws down with left hand and back paws with elbow of right arm. Poke pill into its mouth with right forefinger.
4. Retrieve cat from under bed. Get new pill from bottle. (Resist impulse to get new cat.)
5. Again, proceed as in 1, except when you have cat firmly cradled in bottle-feeding position, sit down on edge of chair, fold your torso over cat, bring your right hand over your left elbow, open cat's mouth by lifting the upper jaw and pop the pill in – quickly. Since your head is down by your knees, you won't be able to see what you're doing. That's just as well.
6. Leave cat hanging on the curtains. Leave pill in your hair.
7. Have a good cry.
8. Now, pull yourself together. Who's the boss here anyway? Retrieve cat and pill. Assuming position 1, say sternly, "Who's the boss here anyway?" Open cat's mouth, take pill and… Ooooops!
9. This isn't working, is it? Collapse and think. Aha! Those flashing claws are causing the chaos.
10. Crawl to linen cupboard. Drag back large bath towel. Spread towel on floor.
11. Retrieve cat from kitchen work surface and pill from potted plant.
12. Spread cat on towel near one end with its head over long edge.
13. Flatten cat's front and back legs over its stomach. (Resist impulse to flatten cat.)
14. Roll cat in towel. Work fast – time and tabbies wait for no woman.
15. Resume position 1. Rotate your left hand to cat's head. Press its mouth at the jaw hinges like opening the petals of a snapdragon.
16. Drop pill into cat's mouth and poke gently. Voila! It's done.
17. Vacuum up loose fur (cat's). Apply bandages to wounds (yours).
18. Take two aspirins and lie down.

Women and cats will do as they please, and men and dogs should relax and get used to the idea.

Robert A. Heinlein

PLANS

Commit your work to the Lord, and then your plans will succeed.

***The Bible*, Proverbs 16:3**

The best time for planning (a book) is while you are doing the dishes.

Agatha Christie

PLAY

Play keeps us vital and alive. It gives us an enthusiasm for life that is irreplaceable. Without it, life just doesn't taste good.

Lucia Capocchione

PMT

Women complain about premenstrual syndrome, but I think of it as the only time of the month that I can be myself.

Roseanne

If women ran the world we wouldn't have wars, just intense negotiations every 28 days.

Robin Williams

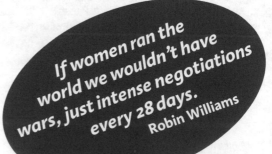

Every "Hormone Hostage" knows that there are days in the month when all a man has to do is open his mouth and he takes his life in his hands. This is a handy guide that could help ease a tense situation ... give it to the man in your life.

Dangerous: What's for dinner?
Safer: Can I help you with dinner?
Safest: Where would you like to go for dinner?
Ultrasafe: Have some chocolate!

Dangerous: Are you wearing *that*?
Safer: You look good in brown.
Safest: Wow! Look at you!
Ultrasafe: Have some chocolate!

Dangerous: What are you so worked up about?
Safer: It's not worth the emotional energy.
Safest: Come here and have a hug.
Ultrasafe: Have some chocolate!

Dangerous: Should you be eating that?
Safer: You know, there are a lot of apples left.
Safest: Can I get you a glass of wine with that?
Ultrasafe: Have some chocolate!

Dangerous: What did you *do* all day?
Safer: I hope you didn't overdo it today.
Safest: I've always loved you in that outfit.
Ultrasafe: Have some chocolate!

Genuine politics – even politics worthy of the name – the only politics I am willing to devote myself to – is simply a matter of serving those around us: serving the community and serving those who will come after us. Its deepest roots are moral because it is a responsibility expressed through action, to and for the whole.

Vaclav Havel

Every political good carried to the extreme must be productive of evil.

Mary Wollstonecraft (1792)

Women need to see ourselves as individuals capable of creating change. That is what political and economic power is all about: having a voice, being able to shape the future.

Madeleine Kunin

No one sex can govern alone. I believe that one of the reasons why civilisation has failed so lamentably is that it has had one-sided government.

Nancy Astor

POSSESSIONS

Possessions are not given that we may rely on them and glory in them but that we may use them and share them with others... Our possessions should be in our hands, not in our hearts.

Martin Luther

Enjoy what you have rather than desiring what you don't have.Just dreaming about nice things is meaningless;It's like chasing the wind.

***The Bible*, Ecclesiastes 6:9**

The more you've got, the more you've got to take care of.

Alice K. Dorman

Until you make peace with who you are, you'll never be content with what you have.

Doris Mortman

POWER

I do not wish women to have power over men, but over themselves.

Mary Wollstonecraft (1792)

Being powerful is like being a lady. If you have to tell people you are, you aren't.

Margaret Thatcher

The beauty of empowering others is that your own power is not diminished in the process.

Barbara Colorose

Prayer enlarges the heart until it is capable of containing God's gift of himself.

Mother Teresa

Is prayer your steering wheel or your spare tyre?

Corrie ten Boom

Prayer is the place where burdens change shoulders.

Source unknown

A modern parable about prayer

A large ship was wrecked during a storm and only two men survived and swam to a desert island. The two survivors looked around them and realised they had no recourse except to pray to God. To find out whose prayer was more powerful, they agreed to divide the territory between them and stay on opposite sides of the island.

The first thing they prayed for was food. The next morning the first man saw a fruit-bearing tree on his side of the island and was able to eat fruit. The other man's piece of land was barren.

After a week the first man became lonely and decided to pray for a wife. The next day, a ship was wrecked, and the only survivor was a woman, who swam to his side of the island. On the other side of the island there was nothing.

Soon the first man prayed for a house, clothes and more food. The next day, by some miracle, all these things were provided for him and the woman. However, the second man received nothing.

Finally the first man prayed for a ship so that he and his wife could leave the island and return to civilisation. In the morning, a ship was anchored off his side of the island, and the crew were waving at him.

The first man and his wife boarded the ship and decided to leave the second man on the island. They considered him unworthy to receive God's blessings because none of his prayers had been answered.

As the ship began to leave, a voice boomed from heaven, saying, "Why are you leaving your companion on the island?"

"These blessings are mine alone," said the first man, "because I was the one who prayed for them. His prayers were not answered, but mine were, so he doesn't deserve anything."

"You are completely mistaken," said God. "He had only one prayer, which I answered. If it hadn't been for his prayer, you would have received none of the things that you did. He prayed that all your prayers would be answered."

PRAYERS

Lord, prepare me for what you are preparing for me.
Corrie ten Boom

Search me, O God, and know my heart;
Test me and know my thoughts.
Point out anything in me that offends you,
And lead me along the path of everlasting life.
***The Bible*, Psalm 139:23–24**

PREJUDICE

Prejudices, it is well known, are most difficult to eradicate from the heart whose soil has never been loosened or fertilised by education; they grow there, firm as weeds among rocks.
Charlotte Brontë

Bias has to be taught. If you hear your parents downgrading women or people of different backgrounds, why, you are going to do that.
Barbara Bush

PRESENT MOMENT

Life is a succession of moments. To live each one is to succeed.
Corita Kent

We don't have an eternity to realise our dreams – only the time we are here.
Susan L. Taylor

Oh, if at every moment of our lives we could know the consequences of some of the utterings, thoughts and deeds that seem so trivial and unimportant at the time! And should we not conclude from such examples that there is no such thing in life as unimportant moments devoid of meaning for the future?

Isabelle Eberhardt, *The Passionate Nomad*

The golden moments in the stream of life rush past us, and we see nothing but sand; the angels come to visit us, and we only know them when they are gone.

George Eliot

Living in the moment means letting go of the past and not waiting for the future. It means living your life consciously, aware that each moment you breathe is a gift.

Oprah Winfrey

Normal day, let me be aware of the treasure you are. Let me learn from you, love you, bless you before you depart. Let me not pass you by in quest of some rare and perfect tomorrow. Let me hold you while I may, for it may not always be so.

Mary Jean Iorn

REALITY

Both abundance and lack exist simultaneously in our lives, as parallel realities. It is always our conscious choice which secret garden we will tend ... when we choose not to focus on what is missing from our lives but are grateful for the abundance that's present – love, health, family, friends, work, the joys of nature and personal pursuits that bring us pleasure – the wasteland of illusion falls away and we experience heaven on earth.

Sarah Ban Breathnach

If you can't solve it, it's not a problem – it's reality.

Barbara Colorose

Reality is something you rise above.

Liza Minnelli

The earth which sustains humanity must not be injured, it must not be destroyed.

Abbess Hildegard of Bingen (1098–1179)

Becoming responsible adults is no longer a matter of whether children hang up their pyjamas or put dirty towels in the laundry basket, but whether they care about themselves and others – and whether they see everyday chores as related to how we treat this planet.

Eda Leshan

We are living beyond our means. As a people, we have developed a life style that is draining the earth of its priceless and irreplaceable resources without regard for the future of our children and people all around the world.

Margaret Mead (1901–1978)

Did you know that...?

Every year over 6 billion drinks cans and 12 billion food cans are thrown away in the UK. How many of those are you recycling?

There's no doing
without some ruing.
Sigrid Unset, *The Bridal Wreath*

*Make it a rule of life never to
regret and never to look back.
Regret is an appalling waste
of energy, you can't build on
it; it's only good for
wallowing in.*
Katherine Mansfield

You will never regret ...

...thinking before acting,
...hearing before judging,
...forgiving your enemies,
...being candid and frank,
...helping a fallen brother or sister,
...being honest in business,
...thinking before speaking,
...being loyal to your church,
...standing by your principles,
...stopping your ears to gossip,
...bridling a slanderous tongue,
...harbouring only pure thoughts,
...sympathising with the afflicted,
...being courteous and kind to all.
Anon.

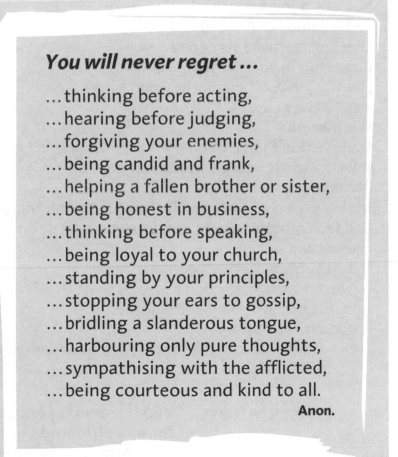

Everyone seems normal... until you get to know them.

Anon.

We control 50% of a relationship. We influence 100% of it.

Barbara Colorose

What I've learned...

I've learned –
that there are people who love you dearly,
but just don't know how to show it.
I've learned –
that just because someone
doesn't love you the way you want
them to, doesn't mean they don't love
you all they can.
I've learned –
that we don't have to change friends
if we understand that friends change.
I've learned –
that two people can look at the exact same thing
and see something totally different.
I've learned –
that just because two people argue,
it doesn't mean they don't love each other.
And just because they don't argue,
it doesn't mean they do.

Source unknown

Love and respect are the most important aspects of all relationships.

Jodie Foster

The five most essential words for a healthy and vital relationship are: "I apologise" and "You are right".

Source unknown

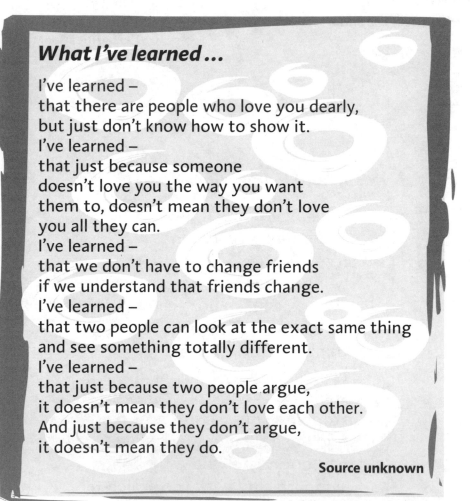

RELIGION

God wants spiritual fruit…not religious nuts.

Ethel Wilcox

Does being born into a Christian family make one a Christian? No! God has no grandchildren.

Corrie ten Boom, *Each New Day*

Some people treat God like they treat a lawyer… they only go to him when they are in trouble.

Anon.

REMEMBER

Twelve things to remember:

1. the value of time
2. the success of perseverance
3. the pleasure of working
4. the dignity of simplicity
5. the worth of character
6. the power of kindness
7. the influence of example
8. the obligation of duty
9. the wisdom of economy
10. the virtue of patience
11. the improvement of talent
12. the joy of originating.

Anon.

REPUTATION

Cautious, careful people, always casting about to preserve their reputations... can never effect a reform.
Susan B. Anthony

Choose a good reputation over good riches, for being held in high esteem is better than having silver or gold.
***The Bible*, Proverbs 22:1**

RESPECT

Respect ... is appreciation of the separateness of the other person, of the ways in which he or she is unique.
Annie Gottlieb

When you squash your husband's ideas, you will squash his spirit... Loss of respect is more hurtful to a man than women realise.
Andy Economides, *True Relationships*

Who am I?
I am a little thing with a big meaning.
I help everybody.
I unlock doors, open hearts and dispel prejudice.
I create friendship and goodwill.
I inspire courtesy and admiration.
Everybody loves me. I bore no one.
I violate no law. I cost nothing.
Many have praised me.
No one has ever condemned me.
I am pleasing to those of high and low degree.
I am useful every moment of the day.
I am Respect!
Source unknown

RESPONSIBILITY

Take your life in your own hands, and what happens? A terrible thing: no one to blame.
Erica Jong

Don't try and avoid responsibility by saying you didn't know about it. For God knows all hearts, and he sees you. He keeps watch over your soul, and he knows you knew! And he will judge all people according to what they have done.
***The Bible*, Proverbs 24:12**

"Responsibility" is my response to God's ability.

We must exchange the philosophy of excuse – what I am is beyond my control – for the philosophy of responsibility.
Barbara Jordan

RIGHT

You cannot make yourself feel something you do not feel, but you can make yourself do right in spite of your feelings.
Pearl S. Buck, "My Neighbor's Son",
To My Daughters With Love

RIGHTS

People tend to forget their duties but remember their rights.

Indira Gandhi, *Last Words*

Give up your rights and you will receive greater privileges with God.

Loren Cunningham

Learn to do good.
Seek justice.
Help the oppressed.
Defend the orphan.
Fight for the rights of widows.

***The Bible*, Isaiah 1:17**

RISK

And the trouble is, if you don't risk anything, you risk more.

Erica Jong

Avoiding danger is no safer in the long run than outright exposure. The fearful are caught as often as the bold.

Helen Keller

Follow your instincts – you never know if your ideas will work out unless you try them.

Lulu Guinness, *Good Housekeeping*, June 2003

The biggest risk is to take no risk at all

To laugh is to risk appearing the fool.
To weep is to risk appearing sentimental.
To reach for another is to risk involvement.
To expose your feelings is to risk exposing your true self.
To place your ideas before a crowd is to risk their loss.
To love is to risk not being loved in return.
To live is to risk dying.
To believe is to risk despair.
To try is to risk failure.
But risks must be taken,
because the greatest risk in life is to risk nothing.
The person who risks nothing does nothing,
has nothing, is nothing.
They may avoid suffering and sorrow,
but they cannot learn, feel, change, grow, love, live.
Chained by their attitudes they are slaves;
they have forfeited their freedom.
Only a person who risks is free.

Anon.

RULES

Home rules

If you sleep on it... make it.
If you wear it... hang it up.
If you drop it... pick it up.
If you eat out of it... put it in the sink or the dishwasher.
If you step on it... wipe it off.
If you open it... close it.
If you empty it... fill it up.
If it rings... answer it.
If it howls... feed it.
If it cries... love it.

***The Locomotivator* 37, Sept /Oct 1982**

The second ten commandments

Thou shalt not worry, for worry is the most unproductive of all human activities.

Thou shalt not be fearful, for most of the things we fear never come to pass.

Thou shalt not cross bridges before you come to them, for no one has yet succeeded in accomplishing this.

Thou shalt face each problem as it comes, for you can only handle them one at a time anyway.

Thou shalt not take problems to bed with you; they make very poor bedfellows.

Thou shalt not borrow other people's problems.

Thou shalt not try and relive yesterday for good or ill; it is gone for ever. Give the past to God and concentrate on the present.

Thou shalt be a good listener, for only when you listen do you hear ideas different from your own.

Thou shalt not be bogged down by frustration, for 90% is rooted in self-pity and will interfere with positive action.

Thou shalt count thy blessings, never overlooking small ones, as many small blessings make a big blessing.

The rules

1. The female always makes the rules.

2. The rules are subject to change without notice.

3. No male can possibly know all the rules.

4. If the female suspects the male knows all the rules, she must immediately change some of the rules.

5. The female is never wrong.

6. If it appears the female is wrong, it is because of a flagrant misunderstanding caused by something the male did or said wrong.

7. If the last rule applies, the male must apologise immediately for causing the misunderstanding.

8. The female can change her mind at any time.

9. The male must never change his mind without the express written consent of the female.

10. The female has every right to be angry or upset at any time.

11. The male must remain calm at all times, unless the female wants him to be angry or upset.

12. The female must, under no circumstances, let the male know whether she wants him to be angry or upset.

13. The male is expected to read the mind of the female at all times.

14. At all times, what is important is what the female meant, not what she said.

15. If the male doesn't abide by the rules, it is because he can't take the heat.

16. If the female has PMS, all the rules are null and void and the male must cater to her every whim.

17. Any attempt to document the rules could result in bodily harm.

18. If the male, at any time, believes he is right, he must refer to rule 5.

Source unknown

S

SACRIFICE

Chew on this…

The pious woman knows that it is her call to give birth and bear fruit, and if she should die in the process, she also knows that, in the eyes of God, she is regarded as a martyr, because she not only dies to herself, but also for the sake of marriage and for the fruit of life…

Palladius, Bishop of Sjelland,
Funeral Sermon for Anna (1551),
(translated from Danish by A. Stibbe)

The greatest love is shown when people lay down their lives for their friends.

Jesus Christ,
***The Bible*, John 15:13**

A woman will always sacrifice herself if you give her the opportunity. It's her favourite form of indulgence.

W. Somerset Maugham

Women do not have to sacrifice personhood if they are mothers. They do not have to sacrifice motherhood in order to be persons. Liberation was meant to expand women's opportunities, not to limit them. The self-esteem that has been found in new pursuits can also be found in mothering.

Elaine Heffner

No, there's nothing in my bag today

Today, I did my maths and science,
I toasted bread,
I halved and quartered, counted, measured,
Used my eyes, and ears and head.
I added and subtracted on the way,
I used the magnets, blocks and memory tray.
I learned a rainbow and how to weigh –
So please don't say,
"Anything in your bag today?"
Yes, I played the whole day through.
I play to learn the things I do.
I seek a problem, find a clue
And make out for myself just what to do.
My teachers set the scene and stay nearby
To help me when I really have to try.
They are there to pose the problems and make me think.
I hope they'll keep me floating
And never let me sink.
All this is in my head and not in my bag.
It makes me sad to hear you say,
"Haven't you done anything today?"
You see, I'm sharing as I play,
I learn to listen and speak clearly when I talk,
To wait my turn, and when inside to walk;
To put my thoughts into a phrase,
To guide a crayon through a maze,
To find my name and write it down,
To do it with a smile and not a frown,
To put my pasting brush away –
So please don't say,
"What! Nothing in your bag today?"
When you attend your meetings
And do your work today,
I will remember not to say to you
"What, nothing in your bag?
What did you do?"

Anon.

Children's answers to questions set in a religious studies test:

- **Noah's wife was called Joan of Arc.**
- **Henry VIII thought so much of Wolsey that he made him a cardigan.**
- **The fifth commandment is "humour thy father and mother".**
- **Lot's wife was a pillar of salt by day and a ball of fire by night.**
- **Salome was a woman who danced naked in front of Harrod's.**
- **Holy acrimony is another name for matrimony.**
- **The pope lives in a vacuum.**
- **The patron saint of travellers is St Francis of the sea sick.**
- **Abraham begat Isaac and Isaac begat Jacob and Jacob begat twelve partridges.**
- **The natives of Macedonia did not believe, so Paul got stoned.**
- **The first commandment was when Eve told Adam to eat the apple.**
- **It is sometimes difficult to hear what is being said in church because the agnostics are so terrible.**

SECRETS

There was once a man and woman who had been married for more than 60 years. They had shared everything. They had talked about everything. They had kept no secrets from each other except that the old woman had a shoe box in the top of her wardrobe that she had cautioned her husband never to open or ask her about.

For all of these years, he had never thought about the box, but one day the old woman got very sick and the doctor said she would not recover. In trying to sort out their affairs, the old man took down the shoe box and took it to his wife's bedside. She agreed that it was time that he should know what was in the box.

When he opened it, he found two crocheted doilies and a stack of money totalling £25,000. He asked her about the contents.

"When we were to be married," she said, "my grandmother told me the secret of a happy marriage was never to argue. She told me that if I ever got angry with you, I should just keep quiet and crochet a doily."

The old man was so moved; he had to fight back tears. Only two precious doilies were in the box. She had only been angry with him two times in all those years of living and loving. He almost burst with happiness.

"Darling," he said, "that explains the doilies, but what about all of this money? Where did it come from?" "Oh," she said, "that's the money I made from selling the doilies."

SECURITY

Women, to be truly loving in a relationship and to give their absolute best, need to feel cherished, honoured and taken care of, no matter how successful they are in the world.

Dr Christiane Northrup, "Men, the Menopause and Great Mid-life Sex", *Woman & Home*, May 2003

Security is mostly a superstition. It does not exist in nature, nor do the children of men as a whole experience it. Avoiding danger is no safer in the long run than outright exposure. Life is either a daring adventure or nothing.

Helen Keller

SELF-CONFIDENCE

Self-confidence is so relaxing. There is no strain or stress when one is self-confident. Our lack of self-confidence comes from trying to be someone we aren't.

Anne Wilson Schaef

You have to have confidence in your ability, and then be tough enough to follow through.

Rosalynn Carter

SELF-ESTEEM

God made you as you are, in order to use you as he planned.

S.C. McAuley

I began to understand that self-esteem isn't everything; it's just that there's nothing without it.

Gloria Steinem

People of high self-esteem are not driven to make themselves superior to others; they do not seek to prove their value by measuring themselves against a comparative standard. Their joy is being who they are, not in being better than someone else.

Nathaniel Branden

Inside every woman who's compelled to perform lies a gnawing sense of inferiority.

Janice Nunnelly-Cox,
Foremothers: Women of the Bible

The woman who feels good about herself and her life, who has high self-esteem and is able to see that her own needs are met, as well as those of others, is more able to relate to others in a healthy way.

Grace Baruch, Rosalind Barnett and Caryl Rivers, *Lifeprints* (New York: McGraw-Hill, 1983, p.30)

Self-respect is the key to self-esteem. We cannot hope to feel good about ourselves unless we are living a life that respects our own values.

Gael Lindenfield, *Self-Esteem*

Trying to heap up trophies to prove how worthwhile I am springs from poor self-image. I believe that I am not loved and accepted so I desperately try to fill in the blank with external successes.

Mary Ellen Ashcroft, *Temptations Women Face*, Kingsway (1992)

SELFISHNESS

Our self-will is so subtle and so deep-rooted within our own selves and defends itself with so many reasons, that when we try to fight against it, we manage to lose in the end. We end up doing our own will under many covers – of charity, of necessity, or of justice.

Catherine of Genoa (1447–1510), *Life and Teachings*

A talented trumpeter who toots his own horn winds up playing to an empty theatre. A talented trumpeter who lets others recognise his talent winds up a legend.
Lisa Edmondson

Don't be selfish…
Don't think only about your own affairs,
but be interested in others, too,
and what they are doing.
St Paul, *The Bible*, Philippians 2:3–4

SERVICE

The first duty of a human being is to assume the right functional relationship to society – more briefly, to find your real job, and do it.
Charlotte Perkins Gilman

In every community there is work to be done. In every nation, there are wounds to heal. In every heart there is the power to do it.
Marianne Williamson

This is the duty of our generation as we enter the twenty-first century – solidarity with the weak, the persecuted, the lonely, the sick, and those in despair. It is expressed by the desire to give a noble and humanising meaning to a community in which all members will define themselves not by their own identity but by that of others.
Elie Wiesel

Life is an exciting business, and most exciting when it is lived for others.
Helen Keller

Don't be naïve – affairs can also be emotional without being sexual.

Andy Economides, *True Relationships*

Women do have a sex drive, but it's easily driven underground by a series of knocks.

Michelle Guinness, *Woman – The Full Story* (Zondervan, 2003)

Love-making in your sixties can be sexier than at any other time of your life.

Dr Theresa Crenshaw

Don't use withholding sex as a club to get your own way... this is damaging to your relationship as a couple and can be emotionally disturbing in your sex life.

Andy Economides, *True Relationships*

Did you know that...?

A study has shown that sex is such good exercise, that a man who has sex with *his wife* three times a week cuts the probability of his having a stroke or heart attack in the next ten years by half. However, adulterous sex was found to increase the risk of a cardiovascular accident!

On a trans-Atlantic flight, a plane passed through a severe storm. The turbulence was awful, and things went from bad to worse when one wing was struck by lightning.

One woman in particular began to scream. She stood up in the front of the plane. "I'm too young to die!" she wailed. Then she yelled, "Well, if I'm going to die, I want my last minutes on earth to be memorable! No one has ever made me really feel like a woman! Well I've had it! Is there *anyone* on this plane who can make me feel like a *woman*?"

For a moment there was silence. Everyone had forgotten their own peril, and they all stared, riveted, at the desperate woman in the front of the plane.

Then, a very good-looking man stood up in the rear of the plane. "I can make you feel like a woman," he said. Tall, well-built, with flowing black hair and jet-black eyes, he started to walk slowly up the aisle, unbuttoning his shirt one button at a time. No one moved. As he reached the woman, he removed his shirt. Muscles rippled across his chest as he reached out, his extended arm holding his shirt at the trembling woman, while he whispered, "Iron this."

There is nothing about age that removes the sex drive. But you're probably less willing to put up with unsatisfactory sex as you get older.

Dr Christiane Northrup, "Men, the Menopause and Great Mid-life Sex", *Woman and Home*, May 2003

SEX APPEAL

Sex appeal is 50% what you've got and 50% what people think you've got.

Sophia Loren

SHOES

If high heels were so wonderful, men would still be wearing them.

Sue Grafton

Give a girl the correct footwear…and she can conquer the world.

Bette Midler

Did you know that…?

Kitten heels are considered to be the perfect height for every woman. They add understated elegance, but are comfortable enough to walk around in all day. They make women feel sophisticated, causing them to walk taller and have more confidence!

SHOPPING

Women go shopping for a man

There was a new kind of shopping centre where a woman could go to choose a husband from among many different men. It was laid out in five floors, with the men increasing in positive attributes as you ascended up the floors.

The only rule was that once you opened the door to any floor and liked the look of one of the men there, if you went up a floor to see what else was in stock, you couldn't go back down except to leave the shop completely. Anyway, a couple of girlfriends went to the place to find a man as a prospective husband.

First floor, the door had a sign saying: "These men have jobs and love kids." The women read the sign and said, "Well that's better than not having jobs or not loving kids, but I wonder what's further up". So up they went to see what was on the next floor.

Second floor said: "These men have high-paying jobs, love kids, and are extremely good-looking." "Hmmm," said the girls. "But, I wonder what's further up?"

Third floor: "These men have high-paying jobs, are extremely good-looking, love kids, and help with the housework." "Wow!" said the women. "Very tempting, *but*, there's more further up!" And up they went.

Fourth floor: "These men have high-paying jobs, love kids, are extremely good-looking, help with the housework, and will wine and dine you." "Wow!" thought the girlfriends. "But just think what might be awaiting us further up!" So up to the fifth floor they went.

The sign on that door said: "This floor is just to prove that some women are impossible to please." It was empty.

Ever wonder what all those advertising terms really mean? Take care next time you go shopping...

New – Different colour from previous design.

All new – Parts are not interchangeable with previous design.

Exclusive – Imported product.

Unmatched – Almost as good as the competition.

Foolproof operation – No provision for adjustments.

Advanced design – The advertising agency doesn't understand it.

It's here at last – Rush job. Nobody knew it was coming.

Field-tested – Manufacturer lacks test equipment.

High accuracy – Unit on which all parts fit.

Futuristic – No other reason why it looks the way it does.

Redesigned – Previous flaws fixed – we hope.

Direct sales only – Factory had a big argument with distributor.

Years of development – We finally got one to work.

Breakthrough – We finally figured out a use for it.

Maintenance-free – Throw it away when it breaks down.

Meets all standards – Ours, not yours.

Solid-state – So heavy you can't lift it.

High reliability – We made it work long enough to ship it.

Signs of modern living

1. You just tried to enter your password on the microwave.
2. You have a list of seven phone numbers to reach your family of three.
3. You call your son's beeper to let him know it's time to eat. He e-mails you back from his bedroom, "What's for dinner?"
4. Your daughter sells Girl Guide biscuits through her web site.
5. Your grandmother asks you to send her a JPEG file of your newborn so she can create a screen saver.
6. You pull up in your own driveway and use your mobile phone to see if anyone is home.
7. You buy a computer and six months later it is out of date and now sells for half the price you paid.
8. Leaving the house without your mobile phone, which you didn't have for the first 40 years of your life, is cause for panic and turning around to go and get it.
9. Using real money, instead of credit or debit, to make a purchase would be a hassle and take planning.
10. Cleaning up the dining room means getting the fast-food bags out of the back seat of your car.
11. Your reason for not staying in touch with family is that they do not have e-mail addresses.
12. Your dining-room table is now your flat filing cabinet.
13. Your idea of being organised is multiple-coloured Post-it notes.
14. You hear most of your jokes through e-mail instead of in person.
15. You get an extra phone line so you can get phone calls.
16. You disconnect from the Internet and get this awful feeling, as if you just pulled the plug on a loved one.
17. You get up in the morning and go online before having your tea.
18. You order your weekly groceries on the Internet and end up eating beans on toast because their server is down.
19. You wake up at 2 am to go to the toilet and check your e-mail on your way back to bed.

6

Little Red Riding Hood in the twenty-first century

There once was a young person named Little Red Riding Hood who lived on the edge of a large afforested nature reserve full of endangered owls and rare plants that would probably provide a cure for cancer if only someone took the time to study them.

One day her mother asked her to take a basket of organically grown fruit and a bottle of mineral water to her grandmother's house. "But mother, won't this be stealing work from the unionised people who have struggled for years to earn the right to carry all packages between various people in the woods?"

Red Riding Hood's mother assured her that she had called the union boss and had got a special compassionate mission exemption form.

"But mother, aren't you oppressing me by ordering me to do this?" Red Riding Hood's mother pointed out that it was impossible for women to oppress each other, since all women were equally oppressed until all women were free.

"But mother, then shouldn't you make my brother carry the basket, since he's an oppressor, and should learn what it's like to be oppressed?"

And Red Riding Hood's mother explained that her brother was attending a special rally for animal rights of community.

"But won't I be oppressing Grandma, by implying that she's sick and hence unable independently to further her own selfhood?"

Red Riding Hood's mother explained that her grandmother wasn't actually sick or incapacitated or mentally handicapped in any way, although that was not to imply that any of these conditions were inferior to what some people called "health".

Thus Red Riding Hood felt that she could deliver the basket to her grandmother, and so she set off.

Many people believed that the forest was a foreboding and dangerous place, but Red Riding Hood knew that this was an irrational fear based on cultural paradigms instilled by a patriarchal society that regarded the natural world as an exploitable resource, and hence believed that natural predators were in fact intolerable competitors.

Other people avoided the woods for fear of thieves and deviants, but Red Riding Hood felt that in a truly classless society all marginalised peoples would be able to "come out" of the woods and be accepted as valid lifestyle role models.

On her way to Grandma's house, Red Riding Hood passed a woodcutter, and wandered off the path, in order to examine some flowers.

She was startled to find herself standing before a wolf, who asked her what was in her basket.

Red Riding Hood's teacher had warned her never to talk to strangers, but she was confident in taking control of her own budding sexuality, and chose to dialogue with the wolf.

She replied, "I am taking my grandmother some healthy snacks in a gesture of solidarity."

The wolf said, "You know, my dear,

it isn't safe for a little girl to walk through these woods alone."

Red Riding Hood said, "I find your sexist remark offensive in the extreme, but I will ignore it because of your traditional status as an outcast from society, the stress of which has caused you to develop an alternative and yet entirely valid worldview. Now, if you'll excuse me, I would prefer to be on my way."

Red Riding Hood returned to the main path, and proceeded towards her grandmother's house.

But because his status outside society had freed him from slavish adherence to linear, Western-style thought, the wolf knew of a quicker route to Grandma's house.

He burst into the house and ate Grandma, a course of action affirmative of his nature as a predator.

Then, unhampered by rigid, traditionalist gender role notions, he put on Grandma's nightclothes, crawled under the bedclothes, and awaited developments.

Red Riding Hood entered the cottage and said, "Grandma, I have brought you some cruelty-free snacks to salute you in your role of wise and nurturing matriarch."

The wolf said softly, "Come closer, child, so that I might see you."

Red Riding Hood said, "Goodness! Grandma, what big eyes you have!"

"You forget that I am optically challenged."

The wolf could not take any more of these species-orientated slurs, and, in a reaction appropriate for his accustomed milieu, he leaped out of bed, grabbed Little Red Riding Hood, and opened his jaws so wide that she could see her poor grandmother cowering in his belly.

"Aren't you forgetting something?" shouted Red Riding Hood bravely. "You must request my permission before proceeding to a new level of intimacy!"

The wolf was so startled by this statement that he loosened his grasp on her. At the same time, the woodcutter burst into the cottage, brandishing an axe.

"Hands off!" cried the woodcutter.

"And what do you think you're doing?" cried Little Red Riding Hood. "If I let you help me now, I would be expressing a lack of confidence in my own abilities, which would lead to poor self-esteem and lower achievement scores on college entrance exams."

"Last chance, sister! Get your hands off that endangered species! This is an anti-terrorist-squad raid!" screamed the forester, and when Little Red Riding Hood nonetheless made a sudden motion, he sliced off her head.

"Thank goodness you got here in time," said the wolf. "The brat and her grandmother lured me in here. I thought I was a goner."

"No, I think I'm the real victim, here," said the forester. "I've been dealing with my anger ever since I saw her picking those protected flowers earlier. And now I'm going to have such a trauma. Do you have any aspirin?"

"Sure," said the wolf.

"Thanks," said the forester.

"I feel your pain," said the wolf, and he patted the forester on his firm, well-padded back, gave a little belch, and said "Do you have anything for indigestion?"

SILENCE

The deepest feeling always shows itself in silence.
Marianne Moore

I like not only to be loved, but to be told I am loved; the realm of silence is large enough beyond the grave.
George Eliot

Everything has its wonders, even darkness and silence, and I learn whatever state I may be in, therein to be content.
Helen Keller,
The Story of My Life

There is a time to be quiet… and a time to speak up.
***The Bible*, Ecclesiastes 3:7**

SIMPLICITY

Live simply, so that others can simply live.
Anon.

Simplicity is making the journey of this life with just baggage enough.
Anon.

A little simplification would be the first step toward rational living, I think.
Eleanor Roosevelt, *My Days*

The ordinary arts we practise every day at home are of more importance to the soul than their simplicity might suggest.
Thomas More

It is the sweet, simple things of life which are the real ones after all.
Laura Ingalls Wilder, *Little House in the Ozarks*

I have learned by some experience, by many examples, and by the writings of countless others before me, also occupied in the search, that certain environments, certain modes of life, certain rules of conduct are more conducive to inner and outer harmony than others. There are, in fact, certain roads that one may follow. Simplification of life is one of them.
Anne Morrow Lindbergh, *Gift from the Sea*

SIN

God and sin cannot live peaceably side by side.
Catherine of Genoa (1417–1510), *Life and Teachings*

Let's never be naïve about our own capacity to sin however strong we may fancy ourselves to be.
Mary Pytches, Between Friends

SINGLENESS

I am a little pencil in the hand of a writing God who is sending a love letter to the world.

Mother Teresa

Living alone, though it may not be the state you ultimately desire for yourself, affords an unparalleled opportunity to know yourself, to be yourself, and to develop yourself as a unique and interesting individual.

Phyllis Hobe

It's not a problem –
it's a gift.

Elisabeth Elliot

To dare to live alone is the rarest courage; since there are many who had rather meet their bitterest enemy in the field, than their own hearts in their closet.

Charles Caleb Colton

SMILING

Smiling is infectious; you catch it like the flu,
When someone smiled at me today, I started smiling too.
I passed around the corner, and someone saw my grin –
When he smiled I realised I'd passed it on to him.
I thought about that smile, and then I realised its worth,
A single smile, just like mine, could travel round the earth.
So, if you feel a smile begin, don't leave it undetected –
Let's start an epidemic quick and get the world infected!

Anon.

We shall never know all the good that a simple smile can do.

Mother Teresa

SOCIETY

A community is not likely to be overthrown where woman fulfils her mission; for by the power of her noble heart, she will raise it from its ruins, and restore it again to prosperity and joy.

John Angell James, *Female Piety*

Women are the real architects of society.

Harriet Beecher Stowe

SOLITUDE

Never be afraid to sit awhile and think.

Lorraine Hansberry

What a lovely surprise to discover how unlonely being alone can be.

Ellen Burstyn

Solitude, if rightly used, becomes not only a privilege but a necessity. Only a superficial soul fears to fraternise with itself.

Alice Rice

SPOUSE

Somewhere out in this audience may even be someone who will one day follow my footsteps, and preside over the White House as the President's spouse. I wish him well!

Barbara Bush

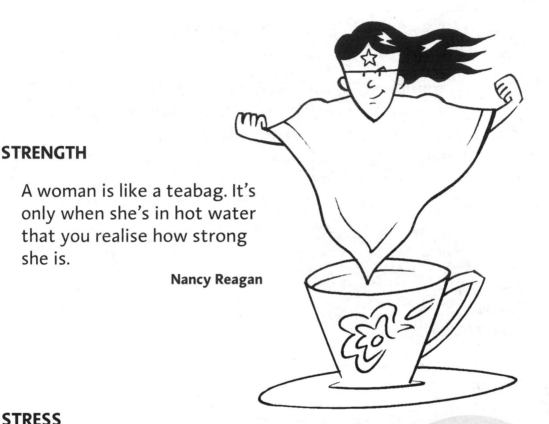

STRENGTH

A woman is like a teabag. It's only when she's in hot water that you realise how strong she is.

Nancy Reagan

STRESS

There was a young woman my grandmother knew,
Who had so many things that she wanted to do,
But just when she thought it was time to begin –
She couldn't because of the state she was in.

Anon.

Listen to your body while it is whispering – when it is yelling, it may be too late.

Allison Pearson, "Sacrifice is written in our Genes", *Good Housekeeping*, June 2003

> *Did you know that… ?*
>
> Tears resulting from sadness, anger, fear or joy vary chemically from those caused by smelling onions and may be nature's method of removing chemicals built up by stress from the body.

STUPIDITY

The great and almost only comfort about being a woman is that one can always pretend to be more stupid, and no one is surprised.

Freya Stark, *The Valley of the Assassins* (1927)

Fools are more to be feared than the wicked.

Christina, Queen of Sweden

I am patient with stupidity, but not with those who are proud of it.

Dame Edith Sitwell

SUCCESS

Top-notch bird

A woman went into a pet shop to buy her daughter a parrot. The owner of the shop showed her a £250 parrot that could use a word processor and a £500 parrot that could program computers. The woman was not satisfied. Reluctantly, the shop owner showed her a £1000 parrot.

"What does this parrot do?" asked the woman.

"I don't know," said the pet-shop owner, "but the other parrots call her 'Boss'."

God has not called me to be successful; He has called me to be faithful.

Mother Teresa

Because I am a woman, I must make unusual efforts to succeed. If I fail, no one will say, "She doesn't have what it takes." They will say, "Women don't have what it takes."

Clare Boothe Luce

Your success and happiness lie within you. External conditions are the accidents of life, its outer trappings.

Helen Keller

I can honestly say that I was never affected by the question of the success of an undertaking. If I felt it was the right thing to do, I was for it regardless of the possible outcome.

Golda Meir

If you find it in your heart to care for somebody else, you will have succeeded.

Maya Angelou

There is no point at which you can say, "Well, I am successful now. I might as well take a nap."

Carrie Fisher

Behind every successful man there's an exhausted woman.

Anon.

If a woman can only succeed by emulating men, I think it is a great loss and not a success. The aim is not only for a woman to succeed, but to keep her womanhood and let her womanhood influence society.

Suzanne Brogger

I attribute my success to this: I never gave or took an excuse.

Florence Nightingale

The seven secrets of a successful monarch:

1. Accept your destiny.
2. Go to your people, and show them you care.
3. Refuse to say anything negative about yourself – be positive.
4. Be wholly engaged in what you are doing.
5. Be philosophical about what others say or print about you.
6. Be yourself, be true to yourself, and make time for yourself.
7. Believe in what you are doing.

Her Royal Highness, Queen Margrethe II of Denmark, interview with *The Sunday Telegraph*, 5 January 2003)

SUFFERING

"I am trying to learn not to waste my suffering."

Sixteen-year-old daughter of Hanley Moule, when dying of TB

A clay pot sitting in the sun will always be a clay pot. It has to go through the white heat of the furnace to become porcelain.

Mildred White Struven

The way I see it, if you want the rainbow, you gotta put up with the rain.

Dolly Parton

Pain nourishes courage. You can't be brave if you've had only wonderful things happen to you.

Mary Tyler Moore

SUPERWOMAN

None of us is Superwoman. We are by turns industrious woman, harried woman, organised woman and sometimes cunning woman, because we all agree that one can always find time, in the most hard-pressed life, to do what one really wants to do, whether it is dancing the tango, playing the harp or writing a book.

Valerie Grove, *The Compleat Woman*

Maintaining a complicated life is a great way to avoid changing it.

Elaine St James

Most people are so busy knocking themselves out trying to do everything they think they should do, they never get around to what they want to do.

Kathleen Winson

TALK

Half the sorrows of women would be averted if they could repress the speech they know to be useless.

George Eliot, *Felix Holt* (1866)

Civility costs nothing and buys everything.

Lady Mary Wortley Montagu (1756)

Did you know that…?

The average woman speaks over 25,000 words a day, and the average man speaks about 10,000.

Gossip and gabble built neither house nor stable.

Norwegian proverb

A gossip is one who talks to you about others;
A bore is one who talks to you about himself;
And a brilliant conversationalist is one who talks to you about yourself.

Lisa Kirk

Did you know that…?

A woman's vocal chords are shorter than a man's. This means a woman needs less effort to speak than a man. Shorter vocal chords make the voice more high-pitched, but also need less air for the voice to become agitated, making it possible for the woman to talk more without using so much energy.

We women talk too much;
Nevertheless, we only say half
of what we know.

Nancy Astor

The generation gap

A teenager: "Mum, you know that china vase on the dining room table, the one that's been handed down from generation to generation?"

"Yes, dear, I know which one you mean, what about it?"

"Well, Mum, I'm sorry, but this generation just dropped it!"

Chain letter for parents of teenagers

Dear Friend: This chain letter is meant to bring relief and happiness to you. Unlike other chain letters, this one does not cost money. Simply send a copy of this letter to six other parents who are tired of their teenagers. Then bundle your teenager up and send him or her to the parent at the bottom of the list. In one week you will receive 16,436 teenagers – and one of them should be worth keeping. Warning: One dad broke the chain and got his own teenager back.

Apron strings

To "let go" does not mean to stop caring,
it means that I can't do it for someone else.
To "let go" is not to cut myself off,
it is the realisation that I can't control another.
To "let go" is not to enable,
but to allow learning from natural consequences.
To "let go" is to admit powerlessness,
which means the outcome is not in my hands.
To "let go" is not to try to change or blame another,
it is to make the most of myself.
To "let go" is not to care for, but to care about.
To "let go" is not to fix,
but to be supportive.
To "let go" is not to judge,
but to allow another to be a human being.
To "let go" is not to be in the middle arranging the outcomes,
but to allow others to effect their own destinies.
To "let go" is not to be protective,
it is to permit another to face reality.
To "let go" is not to deny,
but to accept.
To "let go" is not to nag, scold or argue,
but instead to search out my own shortcomings and to correct them.
To "let go" is not to adjust everything to my desires,
but to take each day as it comes, and to cherish myself in it.
To "let go" is not to criticise and regulate anybody,
but to try to become what I dream I can be.
To "let go" is not to regret the past,
but to grow and to live for the future.
To "let go" is to fear less and to love more.

Author unknown

Parents are wise to overlook seemingly disrespectful outbursts from time to time... the point must be to get across the idea that "I love you always, but sometimes I do not love your behaviour."

Amy Vanderbilt

TEMPTATION

Temptation usually comes in through a door that has deliberately been left open.

Anon.

Temptation almost always assails us at the point where we thought no defence was necessary.

Elizabeth Eton Smith, *Three Eras of Woman's Life*

THANKS

Be thankful for what you have; you'll end up having more. If you concentrate on what you don't have, you will never, ever have enough.

Oprah Winfrey

Silent gratitude isn't much good to anyone.

Gloria Steinem

THANKSGIVING LIST

> **No matter what happens, always be thankful.**
> **St Paul, *The Bible*, 1 Thessalonians 5:18**

Here is a list of some things mothers are most thankful for:

For dishwashers, because they make it possible for us to get out of the kitchen before the family comes back in for their after-dinner snacks.

For husbands who attempt small repair jobs around thc house, because they usually make them big enough to call in the professionals.

For children who put away their things and clean up after themselves. They're such a joy you hate to sec them go home to their own parents.

For teenagers, because they give parents an opportunity to learn a second language.

TIME

The years in your life are less important than the life in your years.

Anon.

Time is a dressmaker specialising in alterations.

Faith Baldwin

The single greatest lament of most people…is lack of time. Often keeping overly busy is a way not to face the uncertainty of stopping and examining where we are going. Time for reflection is essential….

Carol Adrienne, *When Life Changes – Or You Wish It Would*

Eternity is...

... keeping a smile on your face until the shutter clicks.
... waiting for the road-side emergency services to show up.
... listening for the sound of the key in the lock at 2 am.
... trying to find a six-pence error in your bank balance.
... 20 minutes of aerobic exercise.
... not peeping in the oven till the Yorkshire puddings are done.
... awaiting the results of a pregnancy test.
... listening to a six-year-old relate the plot of a movie he likes.
... looking for a motorway exit when you are heading in the wrong direction.
... house-training a new puppy.
... the second hour of Monopoly.
... waiting for the lights to go green when there is an empty parking space on the other side of the crossroads.

after Jane Goodsell

If one sets aside time for a business appointment, a trip to the hairdresser, a social engagement or a shopping expedition, that time is accepted as inviolable. But if one says, "I cannot come because that is my hour to be alone," one is considered rude, egotistical or strange. What a commentary on our civilisation, when being alone is considered suspect; when one has to apologise for it, make excuses, hide the fact that one practises it – like a secret vice!

Anne Morrow Lindbergh

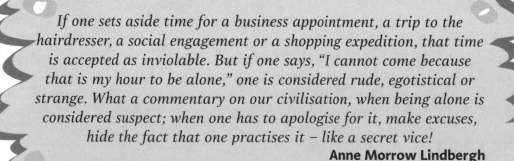

TRANSLATION

Guide to "womanspeak"

She says	English
You want.	You want.
We need.	I want.
It's your decision.	The correct decision should be obvious by now.
Do what you want.	You'll pay for this later.
We need to talk.	I need to complain.
Sure… go ahead.	I don't want you to.
I'm not upset.	Of course I'm upset.
You're… so manly.	You need a shave and you sweat a lot.
You're certainly attentive tonight.	Is sex all you ever think about?
I'm not emotional! And I'm not overreacting!	I'm on my period.
Be romantic, turn out the lights.	I've got flabby thighs.
This kitchen is so inconvenient.	I want a new house.
I want new curtains.	and carpeting, furniture, wallpaper….
Hang the picture there.	No, I mean hang it there!
I heard a noise.	I noticed you were almost asleep.
How much do you love me?	I did something today you're really not going to like.
I'll be ready in a minute.	Kick off your shoes and watch T.V.
Does my bottom look big in this?	Tell me it doesn't.
You have to learn to communicate.	Just agree with me.
Yes.	No.
No.	No.
Maybe.	No.
I'm sorry.	You'll be sorry.
Do you like this recipe?	It's easy to fix, so you'd better get used to it.
I'm not yelling!	Yes I am yelling because I think this is important.

In answer to the question "What's wrong?"

The same old thing.

Nothing.

Everything.

Nothing, really.

I don't want to talk about it.

Nothing.

Everything.

My PMT is acting up.

How can you be so stupid?

Go away, I'm still building up evidence against you.

Guide to "menspeak"

Men don't always say what they mean either:

When a man says, *"It's a guy thing."*
He means: "There is no rational thought pattern connected with this, and you have no chance at all of making it logical."

When a man says, *"Can I help with dinner?"*
He means: "Why isn't it already on the table?"

When a man says, *"OK, sure, darling,"* or *"Yes, dear."*
He means: "Absolutely nothing – It's a conditioned response."

When a man says, *"It would take too long to explain."*
He means: "I have no idea how it works."

When a man says, *"Take a break, darling, you are working too hard."*
He means: "I can't hear the game over the vacuum cleaner."

When a man says, *"That's interesting, dear."*
He means: "Are you still talking?"

When a man says, *"Oh, don't fuss, I just cut myself. It's no big deal."*
He means: "I have actually severed a limb, but I will bleed to death before I admit I'm hurt."

When a man says, *"I can't find it."*
He means: "It didn't fall into my outstretched hand, so I'm completely clueless."

When a man says, *"I heard you."*
He means: "I haven't the foggiest clue what you just said and I am hoping desperately that I can fake it well enough so that you'll not spend the next three days yelling at me."

TRUTH

We too often bind ourselves by authorities rather than by truth.

Lucretia Mott

Any human being can penetrate to the kingdom of truth, if only they long for the truth and perpetually concentrate all their attention upon its attainment.

Simone Weil

There is no art or trickery in a true woman.
She will not flatter,
she will not stoop to humour pet vices,
but fighting and conquering them
she will give her whole loving heart to him
she has thus blessed.

Elizabeth Prentiss

Truth is God's daughter.

Spanish proverb

Father: I want an explanation, and I want the truth.
Daughter: Make up you mind, Dad. You can't have both!

UNDERSTANDING

And verily, a woman need know but one man well, in order to understand all men; whereas a man may know all women and understand not one of them.

Helen Rowland,
The sayings of Mrs Solomon

The most sympathetic of men never fully comprehend woman's concreted situation.

Simone de Beauvoir

We can sometimes love what we do not understand, but it is impossible completely to understand what we do not love.

Anna Jameson, *A Commonplace Book*

To be happy with a man you must understand him a lot and love him a little. To be happy with a woman you must love her a lot and not try to understand her at all.

Helen Rowland

I know I'm not going to understand women. I'll never understand how you can take boiling hot wax, pour it onto your upper thigh, rip the hair out by the root, and still be afraid of a spider.

Jerry Seinfeld

It's little wonder that we as women don't understand ourselves. We have often believed garbled tales about ourselves. For years, if we have turned to psychology or sociology for insight, we have read studies that relate more to male moral decision-making than our own. It would be remarkable if we *weren't* confused about ourselves.

Mary Ellen Ashcroft, *Temptations Women Face*

I wish I could understand women

A man was walking along a beach in California and stumbled across an old lamp. He picked it up and rubbed it and out popped a genie.

The genie said, "OK. You released me from the lamp, blah, blah, blah. This is the fourth time this month and I'm getting a little sick of these wishes, so you can forget about three. You only get one wish."

The man sat and thought about it for a while and said, "I've always wanted to go to Hawaii but I'm scared to fly and I get very seasick. Could you build me a bridge to Hawaii so I can drive over there for a visit?"

The genie laughed and said, "That's impossible. Think of the logistics of that! How would the supports ever reach the bottom of the Pacific? Think of how much concrete... how much steel! No, think of another wish."

The man said OK and tried to think of a really good wish. Finally, he said, "I've been married and divorced four times. My wives always said that I don't care and that I'm insensitive. So, I wish that I could understand women... know how they feel inside and what they're thinking when they give me the silent treatment... know why they're crying, know what they really want when they say 'nothing'... know how to make them truly happy."

The genie said, "Do you want that bridge two lanes or four?"

Top ten things only women understand

10. Why it's good to have ten pairs of black shoes.
9. The difference between cream, ivory and off-white.
8. Cats' facial expressions.
7. Fat clothes.
6. A salad, diet drink and a fudge sundae is a balanced lunch.
5. Finding a designer dress on a sale rail can be considered a peak life experience.
4. The inaccuracy of every bathroom scale ever made.
3. A good man might be hard to find, but a good hairdresser is next to impossible.
2. Why a phone call between two women never lasts less than ten minutes.
1. Other women.

WAR

One is left with the horrible feeling now that war settles nothing; that to win a war is as disastrous as to lose one.

Agatha Christie

You can no more win a war than you can win an earthquake.

Jeanette Rankin

Women will always fear war more than men because they are mothers. A woman will always have a baby, her own or her children's, in her arms. She will always be tormented by fear for her children, the fear that one day she might be a witness to their own deaths.

Natalya Baranskaya

WEAKNESS

Once you can laugh at your own weaknesses, you can move forward. Comedy breaks down walls. It opens up people. If you're good, you can fill up those openings with something positive.

Goldie Hawn

The whole concept that the woman is a weaker vessel is a myth. The point is that they are not... the truth is, they live longer, deal with anxiety better and have babies. In comparison to that, Rambo is a sissy.

Phil Baker, *Letters to a Lady*

Face your deficiencies and acknowledge them; but do not let them master you. Let them teach you patience, sweetness, insight... When we do the best we can, we never know what miracle is wrought in our life, or in the life of another.

Helen Keller

WEALTH

It's better to have a rich soul than to be rich.

Olga Korbut

There are people who have money, and there are people who are rich.

Coco Chanel

WEARINESS

Come to me, all you who are weary and carry heavy burdens, and I will give you rest.
Jesus Christ, The Bible, Matthew 11:28

How foolish and blind are those who choose to cross through the water when the road has been built for them! This road is such a joy for those who travel on it that it makes every bitterness sweet for them, and every burden light. Though they are in the darkness of the body, they find light; and though they are mortal, they find life without death. Or through love and the light of faith they taste eternal truth, with the promise of refreshment in return for the weariness they have borne...

Catherine of Siena (1347–1380), *The Dialogue*

WEDDINGS

Did you know that... ?

Every year, over £300,000,000 are spent on hen and stag nights in the UK. A hen night costs an average of £106, and a stag night costs an average of £215.

Source: Teletext Holiday survey

Men and women have two distinct views about a wedding. The husband-to-be wakes up in the morning, plays a round of golf and counts the minutes until he has to be at the altar.

The wife-to-be, on the other hand, wakes up in the morning and is panicking. She immediately begins to organise things, making sure everything is in proper order. In her mind she is repeating what she has to do.

"All I have to do is go down the aisle, get to the altar, and sing a hymn."

She repeats this over and over again, until she begins to shorten it to three words which she continues to repeat,

"Aisle, altar, hymn."

"Aisle, altar, hymn."

"I'll alter him."

WHAT *DO* WOMEN WANT...?

What the woman who labours wants is the right to live, not simply exist – the right to life as the rich woman has it; the right to life, and the sun, and music, and art... The worker must have bread, but she must have roses, too.

Rose Schneiderman, August, 1912

Women want men, career, money, children, friends, luxury, comfort, independence, freedom, respect, love and cheap stockings that don't run.

Phyllis Diller

What women want is what men want. They want respect.

Marilyn Mach Vos Savant

We still live in a world in which a significant fraction of people, including women, believe that a woman belongs and wants to belong exclusively in the home.

Rosalyn Sussman (Nobel Prize-winning medical physicist)

Often people attempt to live their lives backwards; they try to have more things, or more money, in order to do more of what they want, so they will be happier. The way it actually works is the reverse. You must first be who you really are, then do what you need to do, in order to have what you want.

Margaret Young

A recent survey suggested that a contemporary woman wants:

– to be heard;
– to be allowed to rant and rave when she has a problem rather than being offered an immediate solution;
– her man to tell her when he is hurt, misunderstood or rejected, rather than pretending everything's fine;
– her man to balance love and work;
– her man to notice the little things, even after years of a relationship;
– a man to be willing to risk rejection to get to know her;
– to be shown she is loved by small demonstrations of affection;
– to be made to laugh by a man who is not afraid of making a fool of himself.

When you can't have what you want, it's time to start wanting what you have.

Kathleen A. Sutton

The great question, which I have not been able to answer, despite my 30 years of research into the feminine soul, is "What does a woman want?"

Sigmund Freud

I heard a man say that brigands demand your money or your life, whereas women require both.

Samuel Butler

WIFE

Who can find a virtuous and capable wife?
She is worth more than precious rubies.
Her husband can trust her,
and she will greatly enrich his life.
She will not hinder him but help him all her life.
She finds wool and flax and busily spins it.
She is like a merchant's ship;
she brings her food from afar.
She gets up before dawn to prepare breakfast for her household
And plan the day's work for her servant girls.
She goes out to inspect a field and buys it;
with her earnings she plants a vineyard.
She is energetic and strong,
a hard worker.
She watches for bargains;
Her light burns late into the night.
Her hands are busy spinning thread,
her fingers twisting fibre.
She extends a helping hand to the poor,
and opens her arms to the needy.
She has no fear of winter for her household
because all of them have warm clothes.
She quilts her own bedspreads.
She dresses like royalty in gowns of finest cloth.
Her husband is well known,
for he sits in the council meeting with other civic leaders.
She makes belted linen garments and sashes to sell to the merchants.
She is clothed with strength and dignity,
and laughs with no fear of the future.
When she speaks, her words are wise,
and kindness is the rule when she gives instructions.
She carefully watches all that goes on in her household
and does not have to bear the consequences of laziness.
Her children stand and bless her.
Her husband praises her:
"There are many virtuous women in the world,
but you surpass them all!"
Charm is deceptive, and beauty does not last;
but a woman who fears the Lord will be greatly praised.

***The Bible*, Proverbs 31:10–30**

> An advertisement appeared in a newspaper lonely-hearts column:
>
> *"Farmer wants to marry woman, 35, with tractor.
> Send picture of tractor."*

WOMAN

There are people fond of saying that women are the weaker vessels. I don't believe it! Physically they may be, but spiritually, morally, religiously and in faith, what man can match a woman who is really convinced?

Joseph F. Smith

I don't know how we survived so many years thinking of women as a separate chapter. We are not a separate chapter. We are half the book.
Rosario Green, Mexico's Secretary of Foreign Relations

We are women, and my plea is, "Let me be a woman, holy through and through, asking for nothing but what God wants to give me, receiving with both hands and with all my heart whatever that is."
Elisabeth Elliot

Women's place is where they can do the most good.
Esther Peterson

As a woman I have no country. As a woman my country is the whole world.

Virginia Woolf

One is not born, but rather becomes a woman.
Simone de Beauvoir, *The Second Sex*

And God made woman...

By the time the Lord made woman, he was into his sixth day of working overtime. An angel appeared and said, "Why are you spending so much time on this one?"

And the Lord answered and said, "Have you seen the spec sheet on her? She has to be completely washable, but not plastic, have 200 movable parts, all replaceable, run on black coffee and leftovers, have a lap that can hold three children at one time, have a kiss that can cure anything from a scraped knee to a broken heart, and have six pairs of hands."

The angel tried to stop the Lord. "This is too much work for one day. Wait until tomorrow to finish."

"But I can't!" the Lord protested. "I am so close to finishing this creation that is so close to my own heart. She already heals herself when she is sick *and* can work 18-hour days."

The angel moved closer and touched the woman. "But you have made her so soft, Lord."

"She is soft," the Lord agreed, "but I have also made her tough. You have no idea what she can endure or accomplish."

"Will she be able to think?" asked the angel. The Lord replied, "Not only will she be able to think, she will be able to reason, and negotiate."

The angel then noticed something and reached out and touched the woman's cheek. "Oops, it looks like you have a leak with this model. I told you that you were trying to put too much into this one."

"That's not a leak," the Lord objected, "that's a tear!"

"What's the tear for?" the angel asked.

The Lord said, "The tear is her way of expressing her joy, her sorrow, her pain, her disappointment, her loneliness, her grief, and her pride."

The angel was impressed. "You are a genius, Lord. You thought of everything, for women are truly amazing."

Woman – a chemical analysis

Element: Woman
Symbol: Wo
Atomic Weight: Accepted as 118, but known to vary 105–175.
Discoverer: Adam
Occurrence: Copious quantities in all urban areas, with slightly lower concentrations in suburban and rural areas. Subject to seasonal fluctuations.

Physical properties

1. Surface usually covered with painted film.
2. Boils at nothing, freezes without reason.
3. Melts if given special treatment.
4. Bitter if used incorrectly. Can cause headaches. Handle with care!
5. Found in various states; ranging from virgin metal to common ore.
6. Yields to pressure applied to correct points.

Chemical properties

1. Has great affinity for gold, silver, platinum and many precious stones.
2. Absorbs great quantities of expensive substances.
3. May explode spontaneously.
4. Insoluble in liquids, but there is increased activity when saturated in alcohol to a certain point.
5. Repels cheap material.
6. Most powerful money-reducing agent known to mankind.

Uses

1. Highly ornamental.
2. Can greatly improve relaxation levels.
3. Can warm and comfort under some circumstances.
4. Can cool things down when it's too hot.

Tests

1. Pure specimen turns rosy pink when discovered in natural state.
2. Turns green when placed beside a better specimen.

Caution

1. Highly dangerous except in experienced hands. Use extreme care when handling.
2. Illegal to possess more than one.

WORDS

A great many people think that polysyllables are a sign of intelligence.

Barbara Walters

We live at the level of our language. Whatever we can articulate we can imagine or explore.

Ellen Gilchrist

The kindest word in all the world is the word left unsaid.

Anon.

Small talk is not about facts or words. It's about putting people at their ease.

Leil Lowndes, *How To Talk To Anyone*

Words which do not give the light of Christ increase the darkness.

Mother Teresa

Punctuate this correctly

An English professor wrote the words,
"Woman without her man is nothing"
on the blackboard and asked the students to punctuate it correctly.

The men wrote: *"Woman, without her man, is nothing."*
The women wrote: *"Woman: without her, man is nothing."*

A mother's dictionary

Bottle-feeding: an opportunity for Daddy to get up at 2 am too.

Defence: What you'd better have around the garden if you're going to let the children play outside.

Drooling: How teething babies wash their chins.

Dumbwaiter: One who asks if the kids would care to order dessert.

Family planning: The art of spacing your children the proper distance apart to keep you on the edge of financial disaster.

Feedback: The inevitable result when the baby doesn't appreciate the strained carrots.

Full name: What you call your child when you're mad at him.

Grandparents: The people who think your children are wonderful even though they're sure you're not raising them correctly.

Hearsay: What toddlers do when anyone mutters a dirty word.

Impregnable: A woman whose memory of labour is still vivid.

Independent: How we want our children to be as long as they do everything we say.

Look out: What it's too late for your child to do by the time you scream it.

Pre-natal: When your life was still somewhat your own.

Prepared childbirth: A contradiction in terms.

Puddle: A small body of water that draws other small bodies wearing dry shoes into it.

Show off: A child who is more talented than yours.

Sterilise: What you do to your first baby's dummy by boiling it and to your last baby's dummy by blowing on it.

Storeroom: The distance required between the supermarket aisles so that children in shopping trolleys can't quite reach anything.

Temper tantrums: What you should keep to a minimum so as to not upset the children.

Top bunk: Where you should never put a child wearing Superman pyjamas.

Two-minute warning: When the baby's face turns red and she begins to make those familiar grunting noises.

Verbal: Able to whine in words.

Whodunit: None of the kids that live in your house.

Whoops: An exclamation that translates roughly into "get a sponge".

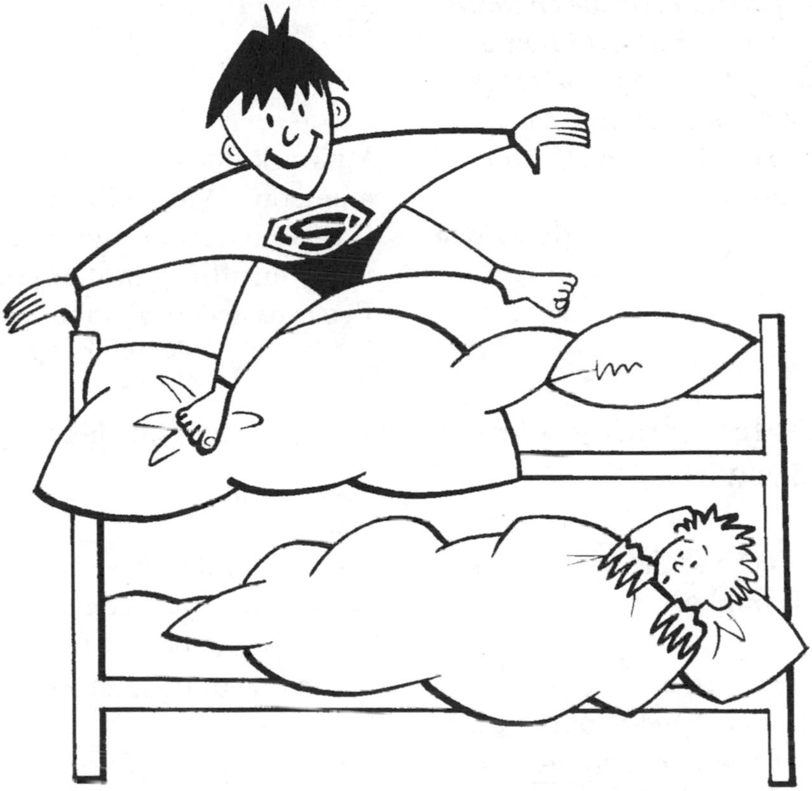

WORK

Let me be clear about one thing. Whether or not you have a paid job, you work.
Marjorie Shaevitz, *The Superwoman Syndrome* (Fontana, 1985)

One who lives long always finds enough work to do.
Norwegian proverb

To *enjoy your work* and accept your lot in life – that is indeed a gift from God. People who do this rarely look with sorrow on the past, for God has given them reasons for joy.
***The Bible*, Ecclesiastes 5:19–20**

Men are allowed to have passion and commitment for their work… a woman is allowed that feeling for man, but not her work.
Barbra Streisand, *People Magazine*, 31 May 1993

At work, you think of the children you have left at home. At home, you think of the work you've left unfinished. Such a struggle is unleashed within yourself. Your heart is rent.

Golda Meir

My work doesn't complete me as a person. What will complete me is a family... that's going to be more fulfilling than anything I've ever accomplished in my life.

Jennifer Lopez, *In Style*

Excuses for working mums to use when caught sleeping at their desk:

They told me at the blood bank that this might happen.

This is just a 15-minute power nap like they raved about in that time-management course you sent me to.

Whew! I must have left the top off the corrector fluid.

I wasn't sleeping! I was meditating on the mission statement and envisioning a new paradigm!

This is one of the seven habits of highly effective people!

I was testing the keyboard for drool resistance.

I'm actually doing a Stress Level Elimination Exercise Plan (SLEEP). I learned it at the last mandatory seminar you made me attend.

This is in exchange for the six hours last night when I dreamed about work!

Damn! Why did you interrupt me? I had almost figured out a solution to our biggest problem.

The coffee machine is broken... and someone must have put decaf. in the wrong pot.

That flu medicine I took last night just won't wear off.

I wasn't sleeping. I was trying to pick up my contact lens without my hands.

Being in your own business is working 80 hours a week so that you can avoid working 40 hours for someone else.

Ramona E.F. Arnett

People who work hard sleep well, whether they eat little or much.

***The Bible*, Ecclesiastes 5:12**

Did you know that...?

The average lunch break is now a measly 27 minutes.

***New Woman*, May 2003**

... the reason women lose out in the workplace over things like pay is that when we get angry over the way we are treated, we cry in the loo rather than direct our fury at our bosses.

Sarah Montague, *Daily Telegraph*, 17 May 2003

The beauty of work depends on the way we meet it, whether we arm ourselves each morning to attack it as an enemy that must be vanquished before night comes – or whether we open our eyes with the sunrise to welcome it as an approaching friend who will keep us delightful company.

Lucy Larcom

Integrate what you believe in every area of your life. Take your heart to work and ask the most and best of everybody else too.

Meryl Streep

You and your boss

When you take a long time,
you're slow.
When he takes a long time, he's
thorough.

When you don't do it, you're
lazy.
When he doesn't do it, he's too
busy.

When you make a mistake,
you're an idiot.
When he makes a mistake, he's
only human.

When doing something without
being told, you're
overstepping your authority.
When the boss does the same
thing, that's initiative.

When you take a stand, you're
being stubborn.
When he does it, he's being
firm.

When you overlook a rule of
etiquette, you're being rude.
When he skips a few rules, he's
being original.

When you please your boss,
you're apple-polishing.
When he pleases his boss, he's
being co-operative.

When you're out of the office,
you're wandering around.
When he's out of the office, he's
on business.

When you're on a day off sick,
you're always sick.
When he's on a day off sick, he
must be very ill.

When you apply for time off,
you must be going for an
interview.
When he applies for time off,
it's because he's overworked.

WORRY

Don't worry about tomorrow, for tomorrow will bring its own worries. Today's trouble is enough for today.

Jesus Christ, *The Bible*, Matthew 6:34

Worry often gives a small thing a big shadow.

Swedish proverb

Worry does not empty tomorrow of its sorrow; it empties today of its strength.

Corrie ten Boom

The worried cow would have lived till now,
If she had saved her breath;
But she feared her hay wouldn't last the day
And mooed herself to death.

Anon.

Worry a little every day and in a lifetime you will lose a couple of years. If something is wrong, fix it if you can. But train yourself not to worry. Worry never fixes anything.

Mary Hemingway

While most of the things you've worried about have never happened, it's a different story with the things you haven't worried about. They are the ones that happen.

Ruth Rendell, *Talking to Strange Men*

Worry is like a rocking chair – it gives you something to do but it doesn't get you anywhere.

Dorothy Galyean

Worry is a cycle of inefficient thoughts whirling around a centre of fear.

Corrie ten Boom

WORTH

An American attorney assessed the monetary value of a wife's services in the home. He listed the various functions she performs: chauffeur, gardener, counsellor, maintenance worker, cleaner, housekeeper, cook, errand runner, accountant, interior decorator, caterer, dietician, secretary, public relations officer, hostess. Using this impressive list of household duties, he figured out the dollar value of a housewife's work in the 1980s labour market was $785 per week, or $40,800 per year. Just think what that would be today!

Too many people today know the price of everything and the value of nothing.

Ann Landers

Who can find a virtuous
and capable wife?
She is worth more than
precious rubies.
The Bible, Proverbs 31:10

Feelings of worth can flourish only in an atmosphere where individual differences are appreciated, mistakes are tolerated, communication is open, and rules are flexible – the kind of atmosphere that is found in a nurturing family.
Virginia Satir

X-CHROMOSOME

Did you know that… ?

There is now scientific evidence that women have been the real movers of society, spreading their genes as they married and moved in with their husband's families. The dispersal process can be traced through female X-chromosomes that have been passed only between females for generations. These show significantly greater distribution and change worldwide than do male Y-chromosomes, indicating women have spread their genes not only from region to region but to other continents, whereas the male chromosomes tend to remain more localised.

Adapted from an article in the *Harvard Graduate Gazette*

YES

Never answer a question, other than a proposal of marriage, by saying Yes or No.

Susan Chitty

Just say a simple, "Yes, I will," or "No, I won't". Your word is enough. To strengthen your vow with a promise shows that something is wrong.

Jesus Christ, *The Bible*, Matthew 5:37

YOURSELF

When a woman feels she has to become anything other than her true self to be lovable, then she becomes less attractive.

John Gray, *Men are from Mars, Women are from Venus*

I'm not going to limit myself just because people won't accept the fact that I can do something else.

Dolly Parton

It is necessary to try to surpass one's self always; this occupation ought to last as long as life.

Christina, Queen of Sweden

Women are always being tested ... but ultimately, each of us has to define who we are individually and then do the very best job we can to grow into it.

Hillary Rodham Clinton

The history of all times and of today, especially, teaches that ... women will be forgotten if they forget to think about themselves.

Louise Otto

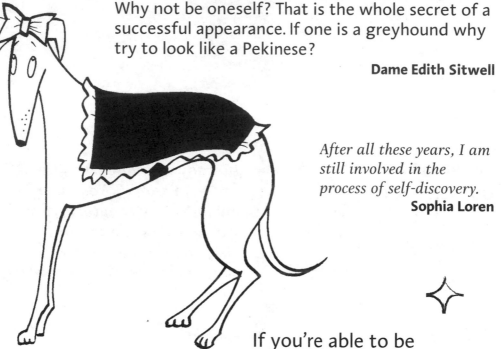

Why not be oneself? That is the whole secret of a successful appearance. If one is a greyhound why try to look like a Pekinese?

Dame Edith Sitwell

After all these years, I am still involved in the process of self-discovery.

Sophia Loren

If you're able to be yourself, then you have no competition. All you have to do is get closer and closer to that essence.

Barbara Cook

You really have to look inside yourself and find your own inner strength, and say, "I'm proud of what I am and who I am, and I'm just going to be myself."

Mariah Carey

The way in which we think of ourselves has everything to do with how our world sees us and how we see ourselves successfully acknowledged by the world.

Arlene Rankin

Youth is not a time of life, it is a state of mind.

Anon.

The excitement of learning separates youth from old age. As long as you're learning, you're not old.

Rosalyn S. Yalow

There is a fountain of youth: it is your mind, your talents, the creativity you bring to your life and the lives of people you love. When you learn to tap this source, you will truly have defeated age.

Sophia Loren

The Lord fills my life with good things, my youth is renewed like the eagle's.

***The Bible*, Psalm 103:5**

In youth we learn;
in age we understand.

Marie von Ebner-Eschenbach

The secret of staying young is to live honestly, eat slowly, and lie about your age.

Lucille Ball

You are as young as your faith, as old as your doubt;
As young as your self-confidence, as old as your fear;
As young as your hope, as old as your despair.

Anon.

Z

ZEAL

Zeal without knowledge is not good;
A person who moves too quickly may go the wrong way.

***The Bible*, Proverbs 19:2**

ZEST

Zest is the secret of all beauty. There is no beauty that is not attractive without zest.

Christian Dior